Mindfulness

Connection

Well-being

Relaxation

Observation

Stress reduction

Anxiety relief

Heart health

Creativity

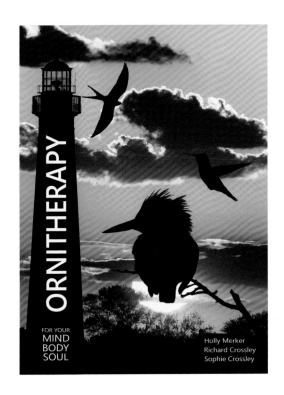

Ornitherapy:

For Your Mind, Body, and Soul

Published in 2021 by Crossley Books
Second Printing
www.crossleybooks.com
www.ornitherapy.com

Photograph credits appear on page 213.

ISBN 978-0-578-82793-3
Library of Congress Control Number 2020925723

Printed and bound in China.

HOLLY MERKER

Holly Merker has a background in art therapy, but today employs birds and nature toward the same goals of wellbeing in her work as an environmental educator. Holly has worked as a professional birding instructor and guide for National Audubon and many other organizations. Passionate about connecting youth to birds, she co-founded the Frontiers in Ornithology Symposium, and has facilitated many young birder groups. Dedicated to bird conservation, she has been state coordinator/reviewer for the Cornell Lab of Ornithology's eBird Pennsylvania. Holly spends every possible moment practicing Ornitherapy, which she credits helping her defeat breast cancer, and restoring her health both mentally and physically.

RICHARD CROSSLEY

Richard Crossley is an internationally acclaimed birder, photographer, and award-winning author of 'The Crossley ID Guide' series. He is also co-author of The Shorebird Guide. Born in Yorkshire, England, he has lived a life shaped by birds, making Cape May, NJ his home for thirty years. His latest book, The Crossley ID Guide: Western Birds, continues to push boundaries and teach people to look at birds differently. Richard also co-founded the global birding initiative Pledge to Fledge, Race4Birds, and The Cape May Young Birders Club. He has contributed to most major birding publications, is frequently heard on radio, and is a sought-after public speaker.

SOPHIE CROSSLEY

Sophie Crossley graduated from The College of New Jersey in 2019 with a degree in Communication Studies and Marketing. She is an avid traveler with a passion for sharing stories through various mediums such as video, photography, and writing. Cape May, New Jersey is Sophie's hometown, though she aspires to use her experience from abroad to intertwine conservation, mindfulness, and freediving to expose a broader audience to the power of nature.

Acknowledgements

It goes without saying that we collectively thank our families, friends, mentors, and teachers for their support and encouragement. We are grateful for their help in building upon our ability to shine our lights outward.

Special thanks to Colleen Cranney and Dr. John Kricher. Their time, expertise, suggestions, and support of what we have aimed to accomplish within these pages was invaluable.

Thanks to Henry Merker for the beautiful artwork on the inside covers of the book.

Others we'd like to acknowledge for their thoughtful input and review:
Diane Bricmont, Jane Butler, Michael Butler, Nellie Butler, Ann Flinn, Diane Fugale, Diane Husic, Pam Steininger Landgraf, Barbara Norris, Kari Oeltjen, Gabrielle Sivitiz, Josh Watts, and Bonnie Yake.

The Ornitherapy Facebook Group was created in response to global pandemic. Thousands of members and contributors shared their stories of what birds mean to them and helped fuel our light – thank you all.

Thanks to the many researchers executing ground-breaking studies that show that connecting to birds and nature promotes mental and physical wellness. Without their dedication, the movements of Ornitherapy and using nature to support wellbeing would have harder hills to climb.

Photography Credits

All of the images in this book were created by Richard Crossley, with the following exceptions. The stunning photo on page 144 was taken by Tony Myshlyaev (@tones.of.blue on Instagram) in Thailand. George Armistead took the photo on page 141. Holly contributed the photos on pages 8 and 89, and Sophie took the photos on pages 27, 36, and 118.

Authors' Note

When a team comes together and is a great fit, they can accomplish things quickly. This book is a perfect example of this, completed in eight fun months of working together.

Sophie, a recent university graduate and avid creator, is the daughter of Richard, an Englishman whose life has been shaped by birds. Holly, an avid birder and educator, met Richard while instructing a teen birding camp years ago. Common conservation goals eventually led Holly and Richard to combining their talents to form two businesses, which has ultimately brought us to where we are now – sharing Ornitherapy!

The creation of this book took a team of multiple talents. The three of us worked together, complementing each other in different ways while simultaneously learning from one another. Holly wrote the Ornitherapy Explorations, fostering the connection to birds and nature through mindfulness, introspection, and good health. Richard shared his all-around knowledge of birds and books, while Sophie cohesively intertwined both the written and visual concepts in the layout and style of the book, allowing a free flow of ideas. Sophie also wrote the Meditation Explorations. Together, we molded the foundations of Ornitherapy.

Now more than ever, we need birds and the natural world. We hope to use this book to bring Ornitherapy to homes, backyards, businesses, health care settings, and schools around the world. Observing birds gives us an opportunity to reconnect with nature, and therein ourselves, in ways many of us have forgotten.

We hope to share our connection to birds with others so that other people may experience the joy and community found within these connections, as well as the mental and physical health benefits they offer. To some, birds are simply another animal. To us, birds are the key to a brighter future.

Let us shed light on our connections and explore them passionately.

Holly, Richard, and Sophie

Ornitherapy
For Your Mind, Body, and Soul

A stressful workload, digital fatigue, constant demands for our attention – life is complicated.

Relief from the pressures we face is critical to healthy living. There's a secret: relief is right outside our own doors. Our minds and bodies need nature. We crave it, whether we realize it or not. It's why we find ourselves daydreaming of escaping to hear waves crashing against the sand, wandering through lush forests, or finding mountains to climb.

We can't always escape on vacations, but we can easily transport our minds and bodies on a wellness journey using birds as vehicles. It's called Ornitherapy, and it is the mindful observation of birds benefitting our minds, bodies, and souls. Science-based research shows that observing and enjoying nature contributes to good health. Using Ornitherapy, we can shed stress and anxiety, which benefits our immune system as a result.

Birds are charismatic and they are everywhere. You just need to look for them. Ornitherapy is accessible to everyone, no matter where you are. It can even be done through your window. Your reward? Focusing on living, vibrant subjects in nature such as birds has been demonstrated to help mitigate effects of any type of stress.

Without any prior experience looking at or identifying birds, you can jump into this book and learn how to look. We will be your guides to connecting with birds and nature just outside your door. Through our Explorations and techniques of mindful observation of birds, you will reap the benefits of healthier living. It will be with you forever and it will change your life.

How to Use This Book

This book is unlike any other you have ever read. If you keep an open mind, the practice of Ornitherapy will teach you to look at birds and nature in context of your own wellbeing, both body and mind.

Ornitherapy is intended for anyone who is interested in the voyage of discovery: discovery in nature, the world around you, and ultimately within yourself.

Again, you do not need to have any experience looking at or identifying birds to benefit from Ornitherapy.

Written to be used right outside your own window or door, this book can be portable or for stationary observation. We believe that focusing on birds already surrounding you is the best way to dial in and learn. This book can also be used in group settings in order to share in community Ornitherapy.

Within this book, there are 58 Explorations and 5 Meditations. At the back of the book, there is a Journaling section that includes personalized notes from each of the authors.

Explorations: Each Exploration was written to empower you to connect with birds and nature in a mindful way using the power of present-moment observation. The Ornitherapy Explorations provide guidance in observation, but also pose many unanswered questions. We believe the voyage in getting to an answer is more important than the answer itself.

Meditations: The Meditations provided are to help you slow down and become mindful of the present moment. Skills applied during meditation, such as awareness and mindfulness, are equally as important in the observation of nature as in our everyday lives. We feel that these meditations are a vital step in connecting to the world within and around us.

Journaling: Taking notes is key to looking closely at anything. The key to getting better is the focus that journaling provides. Use this space to note your observations and reflections.

Throughout the book, we give you the tools and guidance to a structured practice that will help you have a healthier, more productive, and happier life.

Reflecting Through Birds

Through the questions and prompts provided in this book, we invite you to look deeper into nature by first looking inward. Introspection and self-reflection help amplify the wellness benefits of observing birds by practicing Ornitherapy, and taking mindful observation to another level.

There is a misconception that mindfulness must be practiced while sitting in silence and meditating, when in fact, we can practice mindfulness in just about any moment of our lives. There are no special tools required, no restrictions or judgement.

While watching birds and savoring the present moment, you are experiencing a way of practicing mindfulness. This is Ornitherapy. You are in the right here, right now, focusing on what is right in front of and all around you. This practice boosts the wellness benefits of connecting to birds and nature, as well as your sense of self in relation to your surrounding environment.

By observing closely, and asking and answering questions, we can further develop this sense of self-awareness. Ornitherapy aspires to use this contemplation to illuminate how we fit into the greater world around us. By practicing mindful observation, we enhance our experiences with birds and nature, learning more about our personal connections and links to our shared ecosystems. This understanding fosters stewardship.

Harness the power of Ornitherapy. Let birds be your guiding light towards a happier and healthier lifestyle: for your mind, body, and soul.

"When you do things from your soul, you feel
a river moving in you, a joy."
~ Rumi

Ornitherapy Explorations
Can you try them all?

Learning to Look
1

Easing into the mindful observation of birds and nature may seem overwhelming, but is actually quite simple. You are already equipped with all you need to be a good observer and don't need special tools like binoculars or a good camera. Your eyes, ears, and mind will allow you to fully experience the wonders of nature and birds.

Exploring Ornitherapy

• Step outside your door and find a space to explore. This can be your yard, a city park, just about anywhere – because birds are everywhere.

• Make an effort to limit the potential for distractions and interruptions (mobile devices, camera, etc.).

• Slow your pace... Make an effort to walk slowly. Count your steps for one minute in an effort to focus on slowing down. Slowing down allows you to take in more and focus.

• Stay as quiet as possible. Be mindful of your movements and if your body is making noise. Sometimes even our jackets can be noisy, or shuffling our feet in leaves or gravel can be distracting. Birds, like other wild animals, can be sensitive to movement, so moving slowly not only helps your own focus but is less likely to alarm wildlife.

• Find a spot to sit or stand where you can rest for a few minutes, taking in the world around you.

• Practice the art of watching and finding birds:

Look for movement in trees, but also on the ground. Edges of landscapes (where trees meet grass) are attractive to birds. Birds can be fast at times. Most will slow down enough for you to find them and watch.

Birds are motivated by food sources. Thinking about where food might be available, such as trees, shrubs, and sidewalks, is helpful in finding them. Look anywhere with potential for seeds, berries, and especially bugs or worms. Birds also use these places for quick escape from predators and for resting.

The goal is to find birds, not to identify them. Even if you find only one bird, you are successful. If you don't find any, you are still successful because you tried. When you find a bird or multiple birds, focus on just watching. Ask yourself, what do I see?

Devote time to just watching birds for at least 15 minutes. Try and stay focused on birds and in the moment. Let yourself watch the birds.

"The present moment is filled with joy and happiness. If you are attentive, you will see it."
~ Thich Naht Hahn

Getting Closer to Birds
2

It's exciting to get close to any wild animal in the hope of seeing it better: it increases our understanding of what we are looking at and enhances our experience. Approaching birds closely is often a challenge, but if you succeed, the experience is rewarding and memorable.

Birds perceive large animals such as humans as potential threats. The birds become wary and easily flush, which these Eurasian Collared-Doves are known to do. Being mindful of your movements and navigation of your surroundings is key to a close encounter. While others suggest that brightly colored attire will deter birds, we disagree. We believe birds perceive color differently than humans, and that being mindful of our behavior is paramount in approaching birds.

Exploring Ornitherapy

Find a spot outdoors to practice getting closer to birds. Backyards or urban parks are often the best places to start, since birds there are acclimated to people and activity. Think of what scares you. We are all animals and respond similarly.

• Slow down. Birds are hard-wired to respond quickly to movement. Think of moving your entire body into "first gear." No sudden movements: slow motion is the name of the game.

"The goal of life is to make your heartbeat match the beat of the universe, to match your nature with Nature."
~ Joseph Campbell

• Step softly as you walk. This is mindful practice of where and how your foot meets the ground, ever so quietly.

• Remain as quiet as possible. Hush your voice and quiet your breath. Don't forget to turn your devices on silent mode.

• Do not walk directly towards a bird; it will likely flush. Consider different angles that would be less "confrontational."

• Think about where you can best fit into the landscape so as not to be obvious—maybe moving to stand in front of a nearby tree so your shape blends in. This is a tactic used by birds themselves when they want to be obscured.

• Consider lowering your body closer to the ground. This is less intimidating for birds. Sometimes being on your belly works well, depending on your habitat.

• Pack your patience and persistence. It can be hard to do, but patience is ultimately rewarded and will require persistence.

• Sit in one spot and wait. Birds are just like people, becoming less guarded when someone becomes familiar. The longer you sit, the more you will see and understand.

Journal (page 150)

In the Moment: Are You a Pioneer?
3

As a society, we are driven towards expectations of instant gratification and the satisfaction of having immediate answers and reactions. As learners, we've strayed from understanding that getting to an answer by asking questions, and challenging what we think we know, is more valuable than the answers themselves. Being in the moment, having an open mind to explore what's in front of us, allows us to embrace discovery.

In today's world, we're consumed by the digital demands and confinements of structured educations. These mindsets have largely shaped how we look at birds and the world around us. We feel driven to put a name to a bird - to count it, list it, photograph it. But then we often become content to stop there. Do we miss getting to know the bird? What more could we learn about this chickadee featured on the next page?

Immerse yourself in the moment. Take time to question everything and anything.

As pioneers, we recognize that the voyage we go on in learning is the reward. Pioneering minds brought us to where we are now through limitless exploration. Exploration of birds outside our doors is what the concept of Ornitherapy embraces.

Right now, the opportunities for pioneering are enormous. We know so little about birds and nature, in part because we lack the awareness and knowledge of our own surroundings. When we become pioneers of birds, we explore ideas and questions while seeking answers. And we don't have to go any further than right outside our doors to embark on the journey. Are you a pioneer?

Exploring Ornitherapy

• Pick a bird that is familiar to you, one that you see regularly. Ask yourself, how can I get to know it better?

• Unlock its mysteries, allow it to show you who it really is. What is its life about?

• Challenge yourself to spend time with the bird, just like you would a dear friend. Stay present in the moment. Ask lots of questions. You are a pioneer.

"Don't listen to the person who has the answers;
listen to the person who has the questions."
~ Albert Einstein

Bringing Birds To You
4

We all love the beauty of birds. The closer we can bring them to us, the more we learn about and connect to them. There are multiple ways to lure birds closer.

Exploring Ornitherapy

Enhance your experience bringing birds closer by:

• Using tools like binoculars or cameras, or even web and trail cams to zoom in closer. Optics offer us a great advantage to study nature in a more up-close and personal way. Though not necessary for the use of this book, binoculars will enhance your experience and can be found inexpensively, or even gently used.

• Creating an open invitation to your yard. When providing birds desirable habitat (safe places to hide, rest, and nest), you are bringing birds "home." Native plants and trees are the best options for landscaping, providing bountiful food supply and natural shelters for roosts and nesting.

• Sharing a meal by providing food – seeds, suet, nectar, mealworms, or fruit. Bird feeders provide hours of entertainment and allow close observation. Your home will become a bird blind. Scattering seed on the ground or tree stumps is an easy way to get started. There are many different types of feeders on the market, catering to different species. The more diversity of food you offer, the wider variety of bird species you will entertain.

• Offering water – birds need fresh water for drinking and bathing. A shallow dish placed on the ground to provide water is attractive to birds. Dump and refill water each day to keep it clean and deter mosquitos when warm. If you can't offer bird food, this is a great alternative to bringing birds closer.

• Establishing bird boxes – if you have suitable habitat, establishing nest boxes is a great way to share your space with local birds. We recommend placement in areas with a good view and free from roaming cats.

• Window viewing – if you don't have a yard but have a window to view from, there are feeders and nest boxes designed to attach to windows that will give you a front-row view. If you have a balcony, potted native plants with flowers can attract passing hummingbirds, like these Ruby-throated Hummingbirds.

"Adopt the pace of nature: her secret is patience."
~ Ralph Waldo Emerson

Watching Closely: Backyard Drama
5

Like a good movie or television show, watching birds can distract us from what's going on in our own lives, temporarily redirecting our emotions and mental energy. Bird feeding stations set the stage for a front-row view into the dramatic lives of the birds around us, providing us respite and mental recharge from our own hectic worlds.

Bird feeders are not just bird feeders. They become behavior "classrooms," allowing opportunity for intent focus on behaviors, roles, and life-patterns of the birds around you. How a bird behaves while attending a feeder reveals a lot about its personality and how it fits into the ecosystem outside our doors.

When newly arrived, a bird may appear alert or on guard, but after time it relaxes. We see it becoming acclimated to its environment. Birds behave somewhat similarly to people when introduced to new social situations. Think of how you feel when entering a crowd of unfamiliar people.

Notice behaviors through body posture. Note their reactions to other birds and behaviors around a feeder.

Some birds show dominance over a feeder. Impatient, with a "me first" attitude, these birds push others off perches with no apologies. Others will carefully watch the feeder waiting for a vacancy sign and open seat at the table. Some rarely sit on a feeder, instead acting as the clean-up crew, happily scarfing up what falls from the feeders above. Are these birds inferior, or cleverly opportunistic?

And there are bird bullies. Despite their diminutive size, if you have hummingbirds outside your door you will quickly notice their bold and combative behaviors. Feisty birds with an attitude, "hummers" don't let anyone, no matter how much bigger, get in their way. Everyone in their midst needs to beware!

Watch the behavior of the birds at your feeders and see what's revealed about the lives and personalities of your feathered neighbors. Ask yourself, are they much different than the people in your life?

Exploring Ornitherapy

• While watching the birds in your neighborhood, do you notice differences in behaviors between the species you are observing?

• Do some birds tend to feed on the ground or under a bird feeder, versus on the feeder itself?

• Do some of the birds in your yard ignore the feeders altogether, but visit a water feature? This Gray Catbird is enjoying a drink and a bath, but ignoring the suet nearby.

• Look around while the feeders are active. Do you notice a hierarchy of birds lined up and waiting to sit on the feeder?

• Which species dominate feeders? Do some behave like a bully?

• If you were a bird, how would your personality fit into the backyard drama? Would you be a feisty hummingbird, or a wary and quiet Mourning Dove?

"He who feeds a hungry animal
feeds his own soul."
~ Charlie Chaplin

The Jigsaw Puzzle
6

To become more observant you have to look closer. One of the best ways to focus on observation is by transcribing what you see onto paper. Field journaling using words, or sketching the bird, are ways of training yourself to look with intense focus.

Just like when you were in school, taking notes or creating visual diagrams enhance learning and memory.

The best way to get started is by thinking of a bird as a jigsaw puzzle. For example, think of a bird you know well. We chose a Blue Jay. How well can we describe its markings without looking at one?

Imagine this bird in ten pieces, or parts. These parts will be locked together to make a complete bird. Like any good puzzle, you will find it is tough to put it all together quickly. Practicing the "bird puzzle" repeatedly will improve your speed.

The overall goal of this exercise is in focusing on the details. If we look closely at each piece independently, we learn to see more.

Exploring Ornitherapy

Grab something to write on: this journal, a notebook, or even scraps of paper from your recycling bin.

• If you are using a journal, it's helpful to record the date, time, and weather conditions.

• Find a bird to watch. Challenge yourself to make it into a ten-piece puzzle. By using words or sketching it, describe your bird on paper. After you have done this once, try it again, adding five more pieces to the puzzle.

• Continue to make the puzzle bigger, adding more detail and more pieces.

As you keep increasing the puzzle size, you will notice rapid improvement in your ability to see more. Not only will it improve your observation skills with nature, but this will also translate to other areas of your life, like work and personal relationships.

"Let me keep my mind on what matters which is my work which is mostly standing still and learning to be astonished."
~ Mary Oliver

Recording Life: Using Our Digital Companions to Connect
7

We are immersed in the digital era. Screens are constantly in front of us, digital companions to our lives. Enormous amounts of information can be gleaned from these tools, but they are prone to driving us into distraction. We find ourselves constantly negotiating the space and time between the screens, apt to miss natural stimuli surrounding us outdoors. Can we use these devices to our own advantage in connecting to nature, learning more through the power in our palms?

Some would argue that connecting with nature must be pure, without devices or tools. While it's true we need to be mindful of the interference our devices play in our attentiveness, there is some value in using cameras, audio recorders, and webcams in order to learn and connect to nature on another level.

Repetition is the key to learning, and the more you look, the more you see. Can you allow the eye of the lens to help you see more? Cameras, within our phones or slung across our shoulders, can offer us snapshots into behaviors and details too fast or small for our brains and eyes to process and interpret. Most of us have these tools already available to us, and if we use them sparingly, we may be able to get more out of our own encounters.

Recording sounds, behaviors, and instants in a bird's life can be rewarding. We can zoom in to see more, watch repeatedly to understand and discover, or listen closely to recognize patterns.These tools also allow us to share what we see and hear with others, and also document observations for citizen science projects. The benefits outweigh any negatives in learning. And while these 2-D artifacts will never replace real life, they can become useful tools in making deeper connections and promoting stewardship of the world around us.

Exploring Ornitherapy

• Using a smartphone, tablet, or camera, record a video or take some photos of a bird you see outside your door.

• It doesn't have to be portrait quality for you to learn from it. In fact, you can learn a lot about a bird's size, shape, and behavior from a blurry video. Your eyes and mind will not be distracted by color or other details, and instead will focus on other key points like how the bird moves.

• Using the recording app pre-installed on your phone, make an audio recording of the song of a bird outside your door. Play it over and over and draw out how the song "looks" in a visual diagram – upward slashes for notes ascending in pitch, loops for repetition, downward slopes for descending tone. Can you learn songs by creating your own visual diagrams?

• Does using a digital device enhance your understanding and connection with the natural world and birds around you?

"A camera is a save button
for the mind's eye."
~ Roger Kingston

Cortisol and Nature
8

When we step outside our door and into nature, chemical responses explode inside our bodies. Cortisol, the hormone that flips into overdrive when we are stressed, starts to lower. Instantly, our bodies and mind begin to react to the natural connections, triggering internal changes that can improve our wellbeing: emotionally, mentally, and physically. Science-based research shows that connecting with nature reduces our stress levels significantly. And the more we connect, the better we feel – inside and out.

Exposure to nature is now on the Doctor's Orders. A recent study by the University of Michigan concluded that if we connect with nature for at least 20 minutes at a time, 3 times a week, our cortisol levels will be lowered significantly. This is a good thing. This internal chemical warning signal governs stress-reactions in our mood, immune system, metabolism, and the aging process. Excess cortisol in our system makes our body sluggish, and jeopardizes health.

If we dose ourselves with nature, we medicate ourselves naturally by lowering our cortisol levels. As a result, our overall health and disease resistance will improve. Does this mean that by watching birds and nature around us we can improve our health? Research demonstrates that it can. Through Ornitherapy, our bodies become stronger, healthier, and perhaps we even delay the effects of aging – just a little longer.

> *"Nature itself is the best physician."*
> *~ Hippocrates*

Exploring Ornitherapy

• Set aside at least 20 minutes to get outdoors and connect with birds.

• When you start this, take a self-inventory of how you feel.
Are you stressed? Distracted? Tired? Write your feelings down.

• Walk in nature, making connections through mindful observation of birds.
Allow yourself to relax and find enjoyment in the experience. Write down what
you most enjoyed and why.

• In the end, think about how you feel and if the experience left you wanting
more. Do you think nature can help heal you and support your health?

Taking a Walk
9

Even familiar places are worth exploring; they offer undiscovered rewards. With patience and an open mind, you will discover hidden treasures.

Exploring Ornitherapy

Set off on a walk outside. This can be anywhere, even down a city street. It doesn't need to be a long walk to be effective for your body and mind.

Look and listen: Can you find evidence of birds nearby? How many different species can you detect? You do not need to be able to identify them in order to discover differences.

Write down your observations.
- What was the weather like?
- What did you see?
- What other animals did you encounter?
- Did you notice any behaviors that were of interest when looking at birds or animals along your path?

Repeat this same walk tomorrow, retracing your path, and see if you can add more birds or animals to your notes. The goal each time you go out is to find and observe more. With practice, you will tune your brain into nature.

Focusing on the lives of birds and other animals can put things in perspective in our own lives, and center us in ways we may never have noticed.

"By discovering nature, you
discover yourself."
~ Maxime Legace

Journal (page 157)

Know What You Know
10

When we are open to discovery, the realization that we know little is both surprising and exciting. In nature, boundless opportunities for discovery await us.

Exploring Ornitherapy

Select a species from birds you see most often in your area, and can easily study and watch. We used the American Robin shown at right.

This study can be done throughout the course of a day, or even multiple days.

At the start of this exploration, write down the facts you know about it which you have learned through your own previous observation (appearance, sound, behavior, etc.).

Through observation, challenge yourself to add new observations:
- Behaviors
- Patterns of color
- Do the individual birds all look the same?
- Fine details of a part of its body (like the bill/beak or feet)

Ask yourself these questions:
- Can I tell if it's male or female?
- Does it use its tail for anything obvious?
- How does it move? Does it walk, hop, jump, or fly?
- Am I able to tell how it uses its bill?
- Would it be able to fly long distances?

After your study, how many new facts are you able to add to your list of what you know about this bird?

The careful observation of another animal's life helps carry our minds away from our own worries, concerns, and fears – if even for just a few moments. This precious break from our own realities can help us recharge our batteries and put life into a new perspective.

"Thinking is more interesting than knowing, but less interesting than looking."
~ Goethe

"In every walk with nature, one receives far more than he seeks. For going out…is really going in."
~ John Muir

Tuning Out While Tuning In
11

We are all pressured by the stimulus of the world around us, whether we are animals, plants, birds, or fish. The expectations and demands of our attention, whether real or perceived, can suck us in and we often lose focus of our goals. By allowing ourselves to tune out of life's pressures for just a few moments, we can tune into a space that allows our minds to flourish and our bodies thrive.

Exploring Ornitherapy

• Go outdoors – in your yard, garden, or local park, and find a comfortable place to rest for a bit.

• Close your eyes.

• Shut all other noises out and just listen. Fine tune your ears and mind to hear only birds.

• Listen and focus for two minutes, taking mental notes of what you hear.

• Start a journal and write down what you hear.

You do not need to ID birds to make this effective.

Ask yourself these questions:
• Did I hear more than one bird?
• Did I hear more than one type of bird?
• What other sounds did I hear?
• Try to describe one of these sounds in words.

Repeat this again... later today, or tomorrow. Gradually increase time spent listening. See what changes. Do you hear more? Are you more able to focus once you've practiced?

In time, this will come easier. You will hear more. Your mind will find a new peace, and you will long for more connections to the world around you. This is mindfulness through birds and nature.

Journal (page 159)

Meditation 1: Appreciating Our Breath

On any given day, we can take more than 23,000 breaths. Twenty-three thousand! Have you thought about your breathing today?

Most of us never think about our breath even though it is one of the driving factors that keeps us alive. Our organs need precious oxygen to keep them working efficiently in the grand scheme of the body, which makes up our existence. We should take time each day to appreciate the work that our lungs do for our body.

Focusing on breathing can also be a great way to relax, destress, and tune into the present moment. No matter where you are in the world - walking in a park, looking at a bird, or even lying in bed at night - your breath will always be with you. That makes it the perfect tool for practicing mindfulness.

Sometimes our breathing changes when we are tired or excited - like when we see a rare bird! This is a great time to tune into the breath and practice mindfulness.

"Breathe in deeply to bring your mind home to your body."
~ Thich Nhat Hanh

Exploring Mindfulness

Find a place outdoors and get situated in a comfortable position. This could be laying down, on a chair, or even sitting on the ground. If you are sitting, make sure to have good posture – sit up nice and tall!

Let go of the day thus far. We are focusing on this moment, right now. Listen to the birds and sounds around you, and allow yourself to be quiet and observe. What has happened earlier today or your to-do list for this afternoon is not important.

Start listening to your breath:
- Is it slow or fast?
- Are you breathing through your nose or mouth?
- Are you trying to control how fast you breathe?
- Can you feel the rise and fall of your chest?

Focus on the sensations in your body:
- Notice how the air feels as it hits the back of your throat.
- Feel your lungs and diaphragm expand and contract with each breath.
- Observe the breath's rhythm and pace.
- If your mind wanders, kindly guide it back to the focus of the breath.

Are you able to tune into the sounds and sights of nature more clearly after focusing on your breath ?

Journal (page 160)

Behavior
12

As seasons change, so do behaviors in the animal world around us. Bird behavior can be fascinating to watch, especially when the behavior is in response to biological (hormones) or physical influences. Like people, birds have personalities and behavioral traits that are unique to a species. Behavior patterns are useful to learn and study, as they are clues in helping you recognize birds and other animals. Observing behavior of birds can also bring us a sense of mindfulness which can help during times of stress and anxiety.

Exploring Ornitherapy

There are so many different behaviors out there to observe. Here are just a few ideas of things to consider:

Focusing on all aspects of bird behavior, think about how, when, where, and why a particular behavior is occurring.

• Pay careful attention to birds interacting with each other – are they the same species? If so, what does the behavior suggest? Or does a particular bird tend to rarely be seen interacting with others of its kind?

• Behaviors like flocking together catch our eye, but are all flocking behaviors the same? Do individual birds within a flock behave a certain way? Cedar Waxwings, like the pair featured here, are often identified by their recognizable flocks in flight.

• Feeding behaviors vary. Can you notice behavioral differences in the ways birds visit the same feeder, or work over the same patch of grass while looking for food?

• Do you notice any body language when one bird interacts with another bird? Why do you think that bird is behaving this way? Can you learn something about what its behavior means? Is the behavior obvious?

• The language of birds is also part of their behavior. Can you notice certain calls or songs that would attract a mate? Signal territory? Signal alarm?

Studying other animals allows us a distraction from our own lives, and any worries or stress we are experiencing. It can be a temporary recharging of our batteries and resetting of our thought patterns to help us navigate our own lives better.

Consider practicing Ornitherapy when you are feeling particularly stressed or anxious. Even just a few minutes may provide relief.

"Men argue, nature acts."
~ Voltaire

Journal (page 161)

Finding Diversity
13

The world spins and relies on biodiversity. Each system, every community, thrives through diversity in nature. Within biodiversity, each link is an important connector to productivity and success. In the avian world, diversity abounds. When we open our eyes, we can see the niche filled by birds in their required habitats, and our shared world.

Exploring Ornitherapy

In a single day, challenge yourself to find as many different types of birds as possible.

This can be from right outside your door, during a walk, or wherever your day takes you.

Keep a running tally, and see if you can find birds on that list that do the following:

☐ Hop

☐ Continuously flap during flight

☐ Flap then glide

☐ Appear never to flap while aloft

☐ Have an undulating flight pattern

☐ Soar in circles

☐ Climb up a tree

☐ Climb down a tree

☐ Bathe in dust

☐ Drum on wood

☐ Float on water

☐ Dive underwater

What was your "best" observation of the day? Was it a behavior you noticed? An individual bird?

By looking for diversity in birds, we can learn a lot about them and how they are adapted to their habitats. Can we also learn something about ourselves and how we adapt to our environments?

"We only know a tiny proportion about the complexity of the natural world. Wherever you look, there are still things we don't know about and don't understand…There are always new things to find out if you go looking for them."
~ Sir David Attenborough

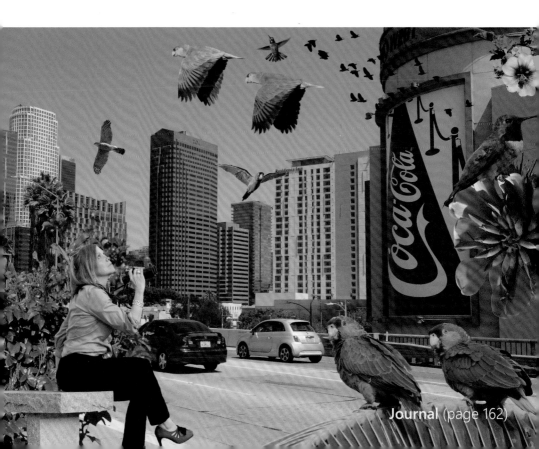

Journal (page 162)

Color in Nature

Color in nature is made up of interactions of light – either playing upon surfaces and reflecting out (structural) or absorbing wavelengths (pigment).

Our lives are colored landscapes. The colors we are surrounded by, assemble and adorn ourselves with, help paint the portrait we live in. We interact with color every moment – whether we see it or not. Color is a constant companion in nature, and for birds changing color is often necessary for survival.

Exploring Ornitherapy

Find a space outdoors, or view from a window.

Look for living things that match every color of the rainbow: Red, Orange, Yellow, Green, Blue, Indigo, and Violet.

Seek out colors in the birds around you.

• How many colors can you see in the birds you observe?

• Can you match the colors of the rainbow with birds in your area?

• Challenge yourself and see if you can pick out multiple colors on a single bird.

• Are there patterns? Do you think the patterns are adaptive? In what ways do they enhance the liklihood of survival of the bird?

Colors and patterns are abundant in nature. When we take a closer look, we might see things we've never noticed before. Think about today: are you reflecting or absorbing the color around you? These Black-throated Blue Warblers wear more than their namesake colors, but how many?

During difficult times, looking to nature can provide us comfort, distractions, and bring perspective amidst changes to the color of our landscape of life.

"The subtlety of nature is greater many times over than the subtlety of the senses and understanding."
~ Francis Bacon

Seeing Red: The Laws of Attraction
15

Flashes of red in nature grab our attention, commanding us to stop and take note. Our eyes are drawn to the contrast of color in our landscapes. Red stands out.

Shades of crimson and scarlet are some of the most compelling and dynamic colors that catch our eyes. This is one reason why Scarlet Tanagers are always a treat to see.

Red ranks as a color that many people deem active and powerful. Red can carry warning and signal danger in nature. But not everything colored with red is perilous. We also consider red to be a symbol of love and life, bold with vibrant energy.

Red birds have long held symbolism for people. Some believe red birds, particularly cardinals, are spiritual messengers. In some cultures, spotting a red bird flying towards the sun brings good luck.

Color is used by people to convey emotion, but also as a tool of communication. We learned this from nature. Birds dressed in red are advertised well and hard to ignore. Some birds only show splashes of red, and are adorned with crimson accents or subtle patterns.

Exploring Ornitherapy

Outside your door, can you easily find shades of red on birds in your neighborhood?

• Can you find a red pattern or patch on a bird outside your door?

• How many different types of birds with red feathers can you see in your area?

• Think about where the red feathers are on a bird's body. How might the color red, located where it is, enhance its success in mating or in survival?

• Could it be an advantage to have red feathers?

• Would you want to be a red bird?

• What's your favorite red bird?

"Nature holds the key to our aesthetic, intellectual, cognitive, and even spiritual satisfaction."
~ E. O. Wilson

Adaptations
16

Nature is in a constant state of change, or flux. And so are our lives. Adaptations are necessary to survival. The body of a bird is uniquely adapted for the food it eats, where it lives, and how it moves around the places it needs to go. These Roseate Spoonbills sport an unusually shaped bill, but imagine how it's used.

Exploring Ornitherapy

Thinking about a bird's body, focus on the bill (beak). Look at the bill of every bird you observe today from outside your door or wherever you go. The goal is to make comparisons.

While looking at the various bills, ask yourself these questions:

• What are the differences in sizes of the bill among the birds you observe?

• How might the bill size and structure be an advantage for a bird?

• How much difference do you observe in bill shapes of the birds you are observing? Do they vary?

• Does the bird's bill inform you about where they live or how they find food?

• How does the bird use its bill?

Like birds, we human animals have adaptations that help us navigate the world around us. Taking time to reflect and focus on the world outdoors can help us adapt to change, and bring us peace during difficult times.

"It is a law of nature we overlook, that intellectual versatility is the compensation for change, danger, and trouble. An animal perfectly in harmony with its environment is a perfect mechanism."
~ H.G. Wells

Journal (page 165)

Goldfinches
17

There are times in life when we could all use some visual treats of gold. Goldfinches are iconic songbirds, offering bursts of bright color onto our landscapes. These tiny songbirds are acrobatic stars of our gardens, often demonstrating showy upside-down feeding techniques as they tweezer tiny seeds from plants or feeders. Their small bodies move through the sky with recognizable bouncy patterns, undulating as if they are skipping through the sky.

Flocking birds, they can be found in large groups diligently combing over seeded flower heads. Goldfinches and thistle go together like bread and butter, the bond between the two mutually beneficial. If you plant native flowers selected from their favorite menu, they will readily accept your dining invitation. These avid songsters warble continuous sweet-pitched phrases, often throwing in unexpected twangs and buzzes, while maintaining an upbeat backdrop to your garden's soundscape.

Watching another animal, how it lives and interacts with the world, can take our minds off our pressures, if even for a short bit. The mental break can help us in ways we may not even have recognized we needed, until we take it.

Exploring Ornitherapy

• Shape: If all birds were silhouettes, how would you describe the goldfinch to someone who's never seen it?

• Behavior: Do you notice interactions between multiple goldfinches? Other birds?

• Patterns of Color: Do they always look the same? Are males and females different?

• Feeding: If they visit a feeder, do they dine casually in one spot for a while, or make quick get-aways returning for one seed at a time? Do they feed in groups or solo?

• Vocalizations: Can you recognize their calls, or songs? The American Goldfinch has a catchy flight call that sounds a little like the exclamation "potato chip!" repeatedly sputtered overhead. If it is in your range, see if you can detect it.

"Sometimes goldfinches one by one will drop from low hung branches; little space they stop; But sip, and twitter, and their feathers sleek; Then off at once, as in a wanton freak: Or perhaps, to show their black and golden wings, Pausing upon their yellow flutterings." ~ John Keats Journal (page 166)

Thinking Inside the Box: Looking Deeper
18

We are all confined to our own boxes, figuratively or structurally. But can we go outside of our comfort zones, and take a closer look at our own worlds, to better understand the bigger picture?

Exploring Ornitherapy

Find a space outside – it can be anywhere. Visualize a box on the ground (around 3 ft X 3 ft). Move yourself closer to the ground in order to get more familiar with this macrocosm.

Use 4 senses to observe:
- ☐ Sight
- ☐ Sound
- ☐ Touch
- ☐ Smell

For the next five minutes, observe this space at the macro-level. Become intimate with it. Study it closely, looking for as many signs of life as you can find.

Ask these questions:
- What signs of life did you observe (even by ear)?
- What patterns do you notice?
- Who might thrive in this space?
- What animals or birds were nearby, or even in this space?

As you repeat this exercise later, expand the boundaries of the box, in turn expanding your mind. The American Redstart (pictured on left) is centered within the box, but what else is surrounding her when you look closely?

Sometimes, it's easy to overlook what's right next to us by looking at the broad and bigger picture. But looking deeper, and closer, into nature brings us new perspectives.

"Look deep into nature, and then you will understand everything better."
~ Albert Einstein

Hummingbirds
19

Dynamic little packages with wings that blur and hum as they move, and feathers that shimmer like tiny gemstones, hummingbirds always capture our attention. The smallest birds on the planet, their size and air agility are an advantage earning them protection from predators. Energetic warriors, hummingbirds have high-strung personalities and spirits to match. They will take on anything in their airspace, especially other hummingbirds. They own their sky.

While tiny, their bodies are designed for energetic performance. To accomplish feats of hover and whir, the hummingbird breathes with ultra-efficiency. Oxygen inhaled instantly converts to blood-energy and is transported to hard-working muscles which drive their life. The hummingbird has a big heart. This large heart beats six times faster than ours in order to sustain a spit-fire lifestyle.

Protein is a necessary building block for any athlete's muscles, and the hummingbird is no exception. Expert bug-gleaners and spider-pickers, hummingbirds are reliant on a protein-packed diet by consuming multi-legged prey. But, the sugary sweet nectar of a flower offers their metabolism jolts of energy required to zing them into their next adventure. They seek the boldly colored flowers we embellish our gardens with, bringing sheer enjoyment as we watch these tiny champions of life.

Exploring Ornitherapy

• Close your eyes. Imagine yourself as a hummingbird, perched on a branch. Do you sit in the shade to blend in, or do you allow the sun to amplify your feathers like glitter?

• Allow yourself to take flight. Will you make a quick escape from where you are? Or hover and watch the world around you as you flutter in place?

• Allow the wind to sail across your body, pushing away your stress. You have freedom. Your fast wings will carry your tiny body anywhere, escaping from the pressures in life. Where do you go?

• Take a deep breath, and slowly exhale... Allow yourself to drift above your world... Leave your stress and anxiety below. Allow new ideas and energy to fill you up, while on the wing.

The bird's-eye view can bring new perspectives to our lives if we allow ourselves to momentarily detach and see things as the hummingbird. We all have wings. We just need to allow them to let us soar.

"We travel not to escape life, but for life not to escape us."
~ Robyn Young

Journal (page 168)

> *"The sky is the daily bread of the eyes."*
> *~ Ralph Waldo Emerson*

Connections to the World Above us: Living in the Airspace
20

Most of us navigate the world around us in the context of terra firma. We have relationships and negotiations with the structures and obstacles we encounter in our daily lives. We surround ourselves by objects of necessity or desire.

Exploring Ornitherapy

Allow yourself to disengage with the objects around you. Let your mind wander free into the airspace above.

Find a quiet spot to sit or stand outdoors, optimizing the widest view of the sky above you.

• Watch the sky for 10 minutes, taking note of anything in flight. Are there are clouds up there? Watch them float by.
• Did you see any birds? If so, did you look at the size and shape?
• Were they all the same, or were some different?

Find peace in the sky, the open space. It's always up there for us, open to explore.

Journal (page 169)

Nuthatches
21

It's easy to adore the nuthatch. These spunky little bark-crawlers can be found busily climbing up and down trees in varied forested habitats. They are the true tree huggers. Like magnets, they scale the bark with powerful cling-on grip, often marching downwards head-first, descending with intent.

These compact-bodied songbirds are well adapted for their bark-clinging lifestyles. Their short tail acts as a built-in brace helping fasten them to the tree. Best known for their craft in hatching nuts, their powerful bill awarded them their name.

Thick-necked and big-headed, their bill is their ultimate tool. Forcefully anchoring a seed or nut into a fold of bark, they "hatch" the nut open by slamming it, earning them a meaty treasure to devour. But nuts and seeds aren't the only thing on their menu. Like detectives, they peer into corners and crevices in the folds of bark seeking hidden evidence. With an inspector's eye, they pick out tiny invertebrates with surgical precision. This is a mutually beneficial relationship:the tree a tool and a food pantry for the nuthatch, and the nuthatch the tree bark's pest manager. Both assist in each other's strength and survival.

This is one example of a mutually beneficial relationship in nature. Like the nuthatches and trees, we all thrive on mutually beneficial relationships in our lives.

Exploring Ornitherapy

• Looking at trees around you, which tree do you think would be the best to "work over" if you were a nuthatch?

• Would you want to scale a tree like a nuthatch? What would thrill you more: walking down the tree trunk, or upside-down on a branch?

• Would you enjoy the thrill of "hide-and-seek" the nuthatch seems to be playing with the bugs in the folds of bark?

• Which mutually beneficial relationships in your life are you most grateful for?

"Trees acquire their strength by growing slowly and flexing with the pressures of nature. Us too."
~ Gene Simmons

Journal (page 170)

Meditation 2: Mindful Movement

As humans, we are always on the go: going to school, going to work, going to run errands. The list of things to do can spill off the edges of the paper, and there are times when it seems like we are zipping around as quickly as a hummingbird.

Birds, like people, have things to do and places to go for their own survival and life cycles. Can you challenge yourself to be still for a few moments? Watch the world move around you while you stay still.

Exploring Mindfulness

Sit or stand outside. Choose somewhere that you will not be interrupted or asked to move. This could be in your backyard, on a park bench, or even somewhere in the city.

First, take a few moments to focus on your own physical and mental stillness. Don't fidget with your phone, hands, or hair. Let your body relax in a comfortable position and bring your mind to focus on the present moment.

Shift your attention to the movement around you.

• What do you see moving?

• Can you hear movement, like running water or wings flapping?

• If you see a bird or animal, how does it move?

• How do birds move compared to humans, or other animals?

• Is there anything that is not moving?

Think about how much more movement you are aware of when you pay attention to the surrounding environment. Movement is around us all the time. Imagine all we can learn from both stillness and motion.

"Nothing is more revealing than movement." ~ *Martha Graham*

Food for Thought
22

Nourishment is a driving force for living creatures. In a bird's life, food availability dictates behavior and forces movement, including extreme limits within the scope of long-distance migration. Diet can sustain bird life, power migration, promote reproduction, and even influence the color some birds display. Birds are hard-wired with intelligence and the mechanical tools to allow them the greatest advantages in finding the highest quality nourishment to satisfy their needs.

People are attracted to watching birds feed. Many of us bring them closer to us for the sole purpose of observation and our own enjoyment. What do we really know about the feeding behaviors of the birds around us? If we take time to observe, we may learn something and gain a new perspective on a species we thought we already knew well.

Exploring Ornitherapy

Outside your door or through your window, focus on feeding birds. This could be at feeders, on sidewalks, on grass, water, or wherever your habitat is. Dine with the birds, invite yourself to their tables.

Ask these questions, and see if you can understand your feathered dining companions better:

• Who are you watching? You do not need to know the name – that's not important to this exercise – just describe them so you remember.

• Where are they feeding?

• What are they eating? Can you tell? Do you think the Red Knots, Ruddy Turnstones, and Sanderlings are eating the horseshoe crabs here, or something else?

• Challenge yourself to identify at least three different items a bird is eating.

• What time of day are they most actively feeding? How do they feed and are they feeding alone?

As we think about how birds feed, we can think about our own nourishment. Ask yourself if you are getting what you need to power through your day. Focus on not just body, but mind and spirit. Can you turn the questions above inward, and learn something about yourself?

"Being in nature nourishes the soul."
~ Eckhart Tolle

Journal (page 172)

Doves
23

Universally recognizable, the dove is iconic in its symbolism for peace and love. But doves are more than just symbols of harmony. They are some of the most ubiquitous birds on the planet, equipped with stellar navigation tools and powerfully fast wings. Because of their abundance, they are arguably underappreciated for their subtle beauty and incredible athleticism.

Pigeon is the name assigned to the larger doves, and many are known for their adaptability to our urban lifestyles. All doves and pigeons have similar body shapes: disproportionately small heads fitted to chunky bottom-heavy bodies and long tails. Their wings can flare wide, but are pointed at the tips, and capable of fast flight. Their flight tactics include excellent navigation skills and mastering speed. Mourning Doves are capable of exceeding 55mph in flight! Possessing a keen sense of direction, it's thought that doves use magnetic fields to navigate with precision across hundreds of miles.

The Passenger Pigeon's sheer abundance at one time, measuring in the billions, illustrated ultimately two opposing successes in nature: thriving and extinction. Spectacles beyond modern-day imaginations, their migrations darkened skies for days, sounding like freight trains overhead. Easy targets, they were hunted en masse, swiftly, and completely eradicated without intention. This is a cautionary tale in the consequences of human impacts and fragility in populations.

In addition to connotations of love, freedom, peace, and spirituality, some people believe that doves are messengers of personal journeys in growth and healing. By carefully watching them, can we learn something about how we interpret the world around us?

Exploring Ornitherapy

Shape:
• Can you identify a bird that is a dove or pigeon easily, just by looking at its shape?

• What feature jumps out at you that tells you that you are looking at a dove?

Behavior:
• Flocking – Do you see doves in groups? If so, are they large groups?

• Flying – How do they fly? Do you notice quick turns while they are in flight? Do their wing beats fast?

• Walking – Doves have distinctive walking styles - what do you notice about how they walk?

• Feeding – Where do doves and pigeons find their food?

"The dove, on silver pinions,
winged her peaceful way."
~ James Montgomery

Weathering
24

A bird hatches into life equipped to endure anticipated weather in its habitat. Withstanding weather is paramount to survival. All parts of the bird's body work together to protect it from the elements of weather it encounters. Birds sense pressure system changes. This allows for advanced preparation of food scarcity and the need for shelter.

Finding shelter is vital during extreme weather. A bird is hard wired to know how to seek shelter for its own survivability. Shelter is often sought in numbers as a group of birds works together for safety.

Can we find community to weather storms in our own life? Are we effective in preparing for changes or slowdowns in our own life rhythms? What can we learn from the birds about weathering our own storms?

"After rain, comes fair weather."
~ Japanese Proverb

Exploring Ornitherapy

In thinking about a bird's response to weather, outside of your door watch for:

Activity:
• Do birds become more or less active right before a storm?
• Do you see increases in activity before a cold night?
• How do birds respond to hot days?
• Do you see groups of birds finding shelter or food in unison, like these Northern Cardinals do?

Body postures:
• Are wings spread open and fixed in place?
• Are they standing on one leg?
• Do they tuck head under wing?

Sheltering:
• Do they position their body into or away from the sun?
• Do they seek shelter in a cavity (birdhouse, tree hole, etc.)?

Journal (page 174)

Nature's Music Therapy
25

Bird songs sound effortless. While song is often a labor of love, it isn't just to attract a mate. Birdsong is generated to grab attention. Does it grab yours?

The soundscapes of birdsong and calls in your local region can be a familiar greeting awaiting you. Listening to birdsong can make us feel relaxed, and sometimes happy. This makes sense, since music activates the part of our brain that releases the chemical dopamine, which facilitates the feeling of pleasure.

Exploring Ornitherapy

Outside your door, challenge yourself to tune into the soundtrack that's "now playing." Thinking about all of the songs and sounds, listen for patterns:

• Repeated phrases and patterns - repetition like the Common Yellowthroat sings, or the patterns of a Red-winged Blackbird song

• Counter-singing (back-and-forth song between two individuals)

• Location patterns – sounds always coming from one spot

• Pitch that is high, pitch that is low

Pick a single individual bird and focus on its singing.

• Does it sound the same each time it bursts into song?

• How much time lapses between each song?

• Does it ever shorten or abbreviate the song?

• Does the song get louder or softer?

• Can you interpret the intention of the song?

One of the best ways to start learning bird song is by creating an outdoor classroom for yourself and learning the birds close to home first. This exercise can help provide you some first steps in listening that can give you an edge when you embark on learning more.

Scientific research shows that heart rhythms can change to mimic whatever music you are listening to. If our hearts do the same for the music of birds, that is a good thing!

"The earth has music for those who listen."
~ Reginold Holmes

Meditation 3: Soundscape Surroundings

We are overwhelmed by a plethora of sounds everyday: cell phones ringing, birds calling, cars driving by, Facebook notifications. How often do you stop to listen to everything that is around you? How often do you notice the natural sounds that are around you?

In order to be able to concentrate, we often only focus on one or two of these sounds. If you are speaking on the phone, you are focused on the voice of the person you are talking to, not the sound of a birdsong in the background.

When we don't focus on the sounds around us, it is very easy not to hear them. We become oblivious. All we have to do is stop for a moment, wherever we are, and suddenly hear a new world of noise around us.

Exploring Mindfulness

Wherever you are, close your eyes. This could be in your backyard, on a park bench, or even at the beach. Take a moment to relax and focus on the present moment.

Notice sounds within yourself.
• Can you hear the sound of your breath?
• What does it sound like?
• What other noises surround your body?

Expand your awareness to your external environment.
• What do you hear?
• Do you hear any birds singing? Is it loud or quiet?
• Can you tell which sounds are close, and which are farther away?
• Notice the sound between sounds - the stillness.
• Does your mind try to label what you are hearing?

At any moment, we can use sound as an anchor to bring us back to the present moment, hearing birds chirping outside our window or the sound of leaves rustling in the wind. Take a listen – you might be surprised by how much you hear!

"There is a way that nature speaks, that land speaks. Most of the time we are simply not patient enough, quiet enough, to pay attention to the story."
~ Linda Hogan

"In union, there is strength."
~ Aesop

Feathers
26

Instantly recognizable as part of the avian wardrobe, feathers are what set birds apart from all living creatures. Together, a collection of feathers adorns a bird to sustain its life – perfectly adapted to its natural lifestyle, providing necessities to survive in many conditions.

A single feather is among a team of many, all elegantly adapted to work together. Delicate yet sturdy, the feather is an intricate work of art. Feathers protect, enable, attract, and repel. Each one has its devoted purpose in a physiological community.

Are we like feathers in our own communities? Are we each playing a role for the greater good of a team?

Exploring Ornitherapy

Think of feather patterns on a bird. Challenge yourself by remembering a bird, and quickly sketching it from memory. Don't use a resource to correct your memory. Try and sketch it as it sits in your mind's eye. Allow imperfection, as perfection is not the ultimate goal. When completed, check a resource to see how your memory recalled this species.

• Think about what you did remember, not what you might've forgotten.
• Think about why you remembered what you did.
• Think about what you forgot; again, ask yourself why.

You might be surprised by the power of this simple exercise. It may lead you to thinking about how you perceive and look at the world around you, and your relationship to it.

Journal (page 177)

Molt
27

Each feather on a bird is uniquely functional and critical for a bird's survival. Birds give their feathers a hard work out. And, like any well-used clothing, feathers will eventually wear out. To keep a bird well-equipped, new feathers will grow in, forcing old feathers out in a process called molt.

When a chick hatches from its egg, like this Killdeer recently did, it begins growing juvenile feathers, which are softer, smaller, and rounder than adults. The feathers grow in fast, enabling the chick to fledge the nest quickly, decreasing vulnerability to predators. As the juvenile bird matures it will need to grow sturdier feathers.

All birds molt annually after the nesting season, a time when life is not so busy and there is plenty of food available. This enables their bodies to devote energy to building and growing in new healthy feathers. Some birds keep these feathers for a year, other birds undergo a partial or full molt in spring. This is typically to help attract a mate or for camouflage during nesting season.

Sometimes you can tell a bird is still "immature" based on the color and pattern of its feathers. The old juvenile feathers, which are worn and faded, contrast with the new fresh-looking feathers. Together, the two different looking feathers create an interesting contrast that demonstrates age.

Molt is a vital process and fundamental in a bird's appearance and ability to survive the rigors of life. Understanding a bird's molt pattern helps us learn more about it while adding a fun challenge to observation.

"When we embrace change, we open ourselves to the understanding that anything is possible."
~ Cleo Wade

Exploring Ornitherapy

Look closely at birds.

• Describe their appearance: do they look dull or bright?

• Can you tell if they keep their feathers for a full year or molt brighter feathers in spring?

• Can you tell if they are young or adult by the feathers they are wearing?

• If you could molt, how would you envision yourself changed?

Molt is a process of renewal and change. Like feathers, renewals and changes can make us stronger, and often help us thrive.

Journal (page 178)

Tails: A Balance of Life

28

When thinking of flight, our minds envision wings; structures that allow freedom, quick escape, and propulsion into distant horizons. But wings have a mechanical companion working in unison to allow flight: a tail. Tails are an integral part of balance – in air, in water, and on ground. Tails allow birds to steer and maneuver, rudders that allow for a change of course when moving. Tails drag in the air to decelerate and slow down for landing. Short tails allow for speed and supreme aerial feats. Tails are anchors, facilitating a climb. Tails play a role in survival of a species – in the laws of attraction. Tails can create "songs" in the wind (hummingbirds), be an array of adornment (peacocks), or a pendulous swing to attract or warn (motmots).

Losing a tail can be costly in a bird's life. Tails are integral to a bird's behavior and survival. The American Kestrel relies on its tail for performance in flight and while perched, where it often pumps it up and down aiding balance.

"Life is a balance of holding on and letting go."
~ Rumi

Exploring Ornitherapy

Outside your door, focus on bird tails.

• Tail Size: Is it long or short?

• Tail Shape: Is it square, pointed, notched, spooned?

• Tail Posture: Can you correlate how a bird holds its tail based on the tail length? How does a bird with a short tail stand, and why? How does a bird with a long tail stand, and why?

• Locomotion: Observe birds in flight, watching only the tail. Watch how it moves or doesn't.

• Take note of birds landing: do they use their tail?

• Behavior: Can you notice behavioral movements of the tails you observe? What do they mean?

A tail is specially adapted to allow optimal functionality in a required habitat. The tail is essential in enabling change. When we look closer and watch, we understand better how nature operates and how we operate within nature.

Journal (page 179)

Wrens
29

Some of the most beautifully complicated, loud, and resonant bird songs in our yards and gardens come from a small, brown, feathered package with a cocked tail: the wren. Wrens, no matter what type – and there are up to 88 species around the globe – all share those common traits, yet can be highly variable in other ways.

People familiar with wrens agree they are full of curiosity, boasting spunky personalities that seem to match a cocked-tail attitude. But despite these traits, wrens can sometimes be hard to find, and are even described as shy. Wrens fill a niche in specialized habitats like wetlands, edges, deserts, canyons, and forests. Others have adapted well to being around humans and are welcomed neighbors in our gardens. They are excellent pest managers, snatching up insects, spiders, and bugs, and helping nature keep its balance.

During the nesting season most male wrens are industrious, building multiple nests, allowing their females to choose their favorite architecture. These charismatic brown birds are entertainers, offering continuous rich songs and intriguing inquisitiveness.

Exploring Ornitherapy

Shape:

- Why does a wren frequently cock its tail? What advantage might it provide for the bird?

- Their bills are uniquely shaped. How are they adapted as a perfect tool for their required diet?

Song:

- Listening to their song, how many times are they repeating a "phrase"?

- Can you hear variation in the song, or do they belt out the same song continuously?

Behavior:

- How would you describe their behavior?

- Do you note anything fun about how they behave?

- If wrens were people, would you want one as your friend?

The Marsh Wren straddling reeds is like a gymnast of the marsh, using vegetation to balance as it navigates its wetland habitat. Have you seen wrens busily moving through small spaces in your neighborhood?

"To be filled with joy by a bird's beautiful song; to be rooted firmly in the simple life, able to embrace the gifts that are there for each of us."
~ April Peerless

Bird Brilliance: The Smarts of Birds
30

The capacity for acquiring and applying knowledge are two hallmarks of intelligence. Or at least that's our human interpretation.

What is intelligence in birds, and are we capable of measuring or understanding avian intelligence?

Crows and other species are known to have sophisticated social structures. Some parrots adopt elaborate vocabularies, stringing words together in sentences. Jays hide food far away, storing it for winter, then fetch it months later. Magpies recognize their own reflections. Ravens use tools and solve problems. These behaviors impress us – maybe because they are feats we can achieve?

Is the real brilliance of birds in the things they do that we are not capable of?

• Migrating thousands of miles non-stop. A young bird's pinpoint accuracy of a thousand-mile journey – with no experience, or "map."

• The "site-fidelity" of the returning hummingbird who clearly knows where the missing feeder should be hanging in your yard, after months wintering hundreds or thousands of miles away.

These are just a few of the unsolved mysteries of intelligence of the bird world. And bird brilliance is really all around us if we take the time to look.

Exploring Ornitherapy

• Can you find bird smarts around you? Which species do you think isn't given credit for its smarts?

• Can you find a clever behavior of a bird outside your door?

• Can you find a mimicking song?

• Have you ever seen birds using tools?

"Human beings are great in their own eyes, but are not much in the eyes of Nature."
~ Kensho Furuya

Flocking: Finding Strength in Community
31

Witnessing the spectacle of a mass congregation of animals in movement can be captivating and mesmerizing. Flocking birds cannot help but to capture our eyes and attention. Gathered animals appeal to the social curiosity of humans, and perhaps even our predatory instincts.

A flock of birds works together: to travel, take advantage of food resources, and assist in security from predators. Flocking can be an asset during migration– one of the riskiest journeys any bird takes. How a flock appears – its rhythm, shape, or pattern of movement – is often a clue in identification. Flocking is a perfect mechanism of teamwork; self-enlisted exertion and participation for the survivability of the bigger team.

During crisis and isolating events, styles of flocking behavior may pause, challenging norms and rhythms of our lives. This forces us to rethink our flocks and shape them differently.

Are there positive outcomes in remodeling our flocks? Will sharing resources and talents in the new flock formation pull us all into better places as a result?

Exploring Ornitherapy

Outside your door, see if you can find some flocks to observe.

Flocks can be in the air, on the ground, atop buildings, on wires, on water – anywhere. Observe the group, but also try and study individuals within.

Movement: How does the entire flock move?

Shape: What do you see?
- A V-shaped pattern
- A large group loosely formed, soaring in a swarm (a kettle of hawks)
- A murmuration (of starlings) that form balls and bunches, choreographed in spell-binding rapidity
- A broken line, a river of birds, or misshapen group

Positioning: Are individuals spaced out perfectly within the flock? Or does it appear that there are no personal space bubbles?

Flocks on the ground: Are birds feeding in flocks outside your door? If so, take note of whether they are mixed species or just one – like American Robins scattered across grass in early spring. Do individuals interact?

Flocks at feeders: Do you see groups of birds attending bird feeders simultaneously? Does it seem that some birds want to be alone at the feeder?

Time of day: Does time of day impact when birds visit feeders?

"Each species, including ourselves, is a link in many chains…when a change occurs in one part of the circuit, many other parts must adjust themselves to it."
~ Aldo Leopold

Reflections in Light
32

Light is powerful. It spellbinds our eyes and mind as we interpret color in nature. It can evoke emotion and affect mood, and helps us navigate within our world.

As diurnal animals, we are adapted to take advantage of the best light the sun has to offer. It guides our daily rhythms and shapes our lifestyles.

The way birds see each other is somewhat different from how we see them. Many avian eyes see ultraviolet light – something we are not naturally adapted to perceive. This dimension of light is thought to be a driving force in mate selection. UV light plays off feathers and shapes how birds appear to one another. We are not privy to these natural signals in light.

If we stop to think about it, perhaps birds aren't really all that meet the eye?

Exploring Ornitherapy

Challenge yourself to observe the interaction between light and birds, and how your eyes and brain perceive it.

• Look for intensity of color that is enhanced by sun or diffused light.

• Does this change your impression or emotional response to a bird you are viewing?

• Find shadows and observe how they change the perception of how a bird appears.

• If lack of light creates shadows, or even just a silhouette, will you still recognize the bird?

• Can you see the iridescence of feathers in the birds around you? What birds come to mind where this striking play of light grabbed your attention?

• What is your favorite time of day to observe birds, and do you think that light plays a factor in this?

"Come forth into the light of things,
let nature be your teacher."
~ William Wordsworth

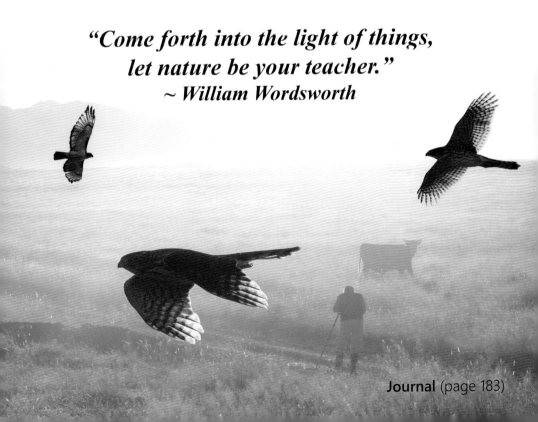

Journal (page 183)

Bluebirds: Harbingers of Hope
33

A gardener's companion, the bluebird is not only one of the most colorful, but arguably the most desired yard resident in North America. Adorned with sapphire blue feathers, folklore deems bluebirds as messengers of happiness and hope.

In addition to their beauty, bluebirds are beneficial neighbors. All three species, Eastern (featured here), Western, and Mountain Bluebirds, provide excellent insect control for our gardens. Bluebirds became scarce due to decline of natural nest cavities. People recognized this problem and then jumped into action to restore populations. Luckily, it worked. With targeted marketing, these cavity nesters can be lured onto our properties with boxes, if nesting habitat is optimal.

In an era where we are constantly reminded of negative impacts we have on our environment, it's equally important to look back at our conservation accomplishments. In your own area, consider ways to change landscapes to benefit native wildlife. Simple practices will lead to thriving habitats for birds and people. Consider selecting native plants and trees to provide ample food buffets for birds and other wildlife. If possible, leave dead trees standing, as they offer natural nesting and roosting sites for birds.

Be inspired and empowered to make a difference for our future generations. Believe in hope.

Exploring Ornitherapy

• Looking around outside your door, do you think the habitat is functional to local birds and other wildlife?

• Could you create or design a natural habitat that supports wildlife?

• What could you change?

"Hope is the thing with feathers that perches in the soul, and sings the tune without the words, and never stops at all..."
~ Emily Dickinson

Journal (page 184)

Dusk: A Twilight Shift
34

At the edge of night, the last stretch of sunlight wraps the world in a soft glow, signaling the end of the day. In the animal world, the bridge from day into night marks a changing of the guard, as dusk gives nod for the night shift to awaken.

In these twilight moments, birds begin falling into place, preparing for their next task. For many this means retreating to rest. Safe spots are sought after in bushes, trees, reeds, or even open water. A trigger stirs in some birds, initiating readiness to embark on a nocturnal long-distance migration. Other birds begin their hunt with adaptations allowing for expert vision in low light. Nature assigns these crepuscular, or twilight, predators a niche to fill in the 'tween light as they hunt insects, rodents, or fish.

There's something special about this time of day. Along with the changing light, nature's soundtrack features songs paired with the light of dusk. Songs of frogs, insects, and birds resound over landscapes. Last light singers like Whip-poor-wills, swifts, woodcocks, bitterns and many species of owl reveal the time of day with no need to consult a clock.

Dusk is a good time to find closure in our day and connect with nature in an intimate way. If we sit, listen, and watch the sky, we will be rewarded. We might see birds flying overhead to a nighttime roost. Or watch a dance in the sky while birds eat bugs on the wing.

Study flight patterns and shapes, as lack of color provides less distraction – the beauty of a silhouette. If we take the time to look and allow ourselves to quiet, the world will awaken around us.

Exploring Ornitherapy

Carve out some time to enjoy this special time outside your door.

The sounds of dusk and nightfall are sealed into our memory. Crickets, birds, and frogs can put us into time and place - like a familiar smell brings to mind a past memory.

What are your favorite sounds of dusk?

Think about a bird behavior you have witnessed at dusk... Were you able to figure out what task the bird was undertaking? Are there any behaviors that stand out or captivate you? If you haven't witnessed any, challenge yourself to find one.

If you have a favorite crepuscular bird, what is it, and why?

"At sunset, Nature is painting for us…day after day… pictures of infinite beauty."
~ John Ruskin

Birds Go Straight to the Heart
35

Do you allow yourself time to slow down and really focus on nature? Being outdoors and connecting with birds and nature is vital to our wellbeing.

We're pushed and pulled in many directions, no matter our age. This can be tiresome, but if we allow birds and nature to slow us down we are self-medicating.

Birds and nature are akin to a drug. Science-based research has shown that positive chemical reactions are triggered inside our bodies when we are exposed to nature and birds. Connecting to nature goes straight to the heart: that is, to our heart health. Studies strongly suggest that spending time in nature can lower our blood pressure. Another reward is a lower risk of cardiovascular disease, because exposure to nature decreases stress.

In this sense, birds and nature are a drug. Do you get your daily fix?

Allow yourself the "guilty pleasure" of really watching. Richard Crossley calls this "bird voyeurism" in nature – taking in the intimate details of another creature's life. Watch how it lives, how it survives.

We can learn so much in these mindful, voyeuristic moments. Our bodies and minds benefit when we dose ourselves with birds.

Exploring Ornitherapy

Allow yourself to be rewarded by simple details, in the obvious and the subtle.

While outdoors, stop and look. Try to be present in the moment. Try not to let life's demands distract you.

Find a spot to safely stand or sit.
- Close your eyes and count backwards from 5.
- Open your eyes and look at the world around you.
- Do a quick inventory of the following:
  What you see
  What you hear
  How it smells
  How your skin feels
- Start to interact with the natural world.

• Challenge yourself to discover three new things: a new sound, a new smell, a new feature on a bird you know well.

Try this for five minutes – see if you can stick to this, and find heightened observation.

Then try it again tomorrow and double your time.

You might be surprised by what happens. Let nature's energy pour into you and fill you up with a natural recharge. This is Ornitherapy.

> ### *"Just being surrounded by bountiful nature, rejuvenates and inspires us."*
> ### *~ E. O. Wilson*

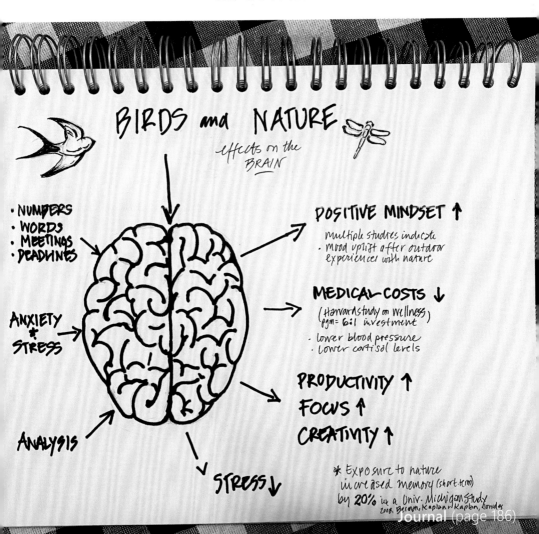

BIRDS and NATURE
effects on the BRAIN

- NUMBERS
- WORDS
- MEETINGS
- DEADLINES

ANXIETY & STRESS

ANALYSIS

POSITIVE MINDSET ↑
multiple studies indicate
- mood uplift after outdoor experiences with nature

MEDICAL COSTS ↓
(Harvard study on wellness)
pgm = 6:1 investment
- lower blood pressure
- lower cortisol levels

PRODUCTIVITY ↑
FOCUS ↑
CREATIVITY ↑

STRESS ↓

* Exposure to nature increased memory (short-term) by 20% in a Univ. Michigan study
2008, Berman, Kaplan + Kaplan, Jonides

We Are Connected
36

All life is dependent on having needs met by surroundings: food, water, shelter, air, and space. These are essential elements of any habitat. Life also depends on balance in the surrounding ecosystems, both at a micro-level or a larger, more global system.

Ecological links are essential for survival. Predator-prey relationships, habitat formations, sheltering needs, etc., are all forms of ecological interdependence.

The relationships in nature are much like our own as humans. We are dependent on each other. Our communities are woven together with needs satisfied by others, directly or indirectly. If we start thinking about how we live, we can see where we are dependent on others for our own survival. More importantly, we are dependent on other species within our shared ecosystems. These relationships are requisite for our survival.

Crisis facilitates a larger awareness of needs. In nature, this could be loss of habitat, food source, or space. As humans, we face the same challenges in crisis. We impact everyone and everything that surrounds us.

We can see that taking care of each other, as well as the links in our ecosystem, are vital to wellbeing of body and mind.

We don't have to look far outside our doors to see connectivity in nature. Stopping to take note of the interdependence of life, and how we fit in, can give us perspective on our own lives. We are linked, for good and bad, to the world around us.

Exploring Ornitherapy

Find a dependent relationship between a bird and another living organism:

• What is the overall connection between birds and other forms of life?

• Do you think a bird's survival is dependent on this relationship?

• Could a bird adapt to meet its needs without this relationship?

• How are you dependent on the ecosystem you are living in?

• Are you physically, emotionally, or mentally dependent on your surroundings?

• Which living organism in your neighborhood do you feel most connected to?

• Which relationship between yourself and something in nature are you most grateful for?

"When one tugs at a single thing in nature, he finds it attached to the rest of the world."
~ John Muir

Journal (page 187)

Living Together
37

Nature hiccups when trying to adapt to human impacts on shared ecosystems. Not all species can conform to survive the change. But occasionally, nature wins from the way we transform habitats and how we shape natural landscapes to meet our needs and desires.

Who thrives amidst these changes? If we look, we can find many animals flourishing among humans. Some birds experience population booms as a result of cohabitation with us and how we live.

You may even see evidence of this right outside your door. Perhaps you cohabitate with some of these thriving birds in your neighborhood? Who are your feathered neighbors that seem to benefit from shared spaces?

Exploring Ornitherapy

• Which birds in your neighborhood do you feel are best adapted to living around people? These feral pigeons seem to thrive among urban areas, so why aren't they everywhere?

• Are there adaptations you notice that give an advantage in survival?

• Who do you think are better at adapting to their surroundings and changes, people or birds?

• What is the most common bird you find outside your door? Do you know why it seems to thrive living among you and your neighbors?

"The earth is what we all have in common."
~ Wendell Berry

Journal (page 188)

Sparrows
38

Spread across every habitat, sparrows are the quintessential little brown bird. Because they spend much of their lives low to the ground, they're attired in plumage matching the earth. Soil, sand, clay, woody plants, grasses, and sedges are the stage backdrops of the sparrow's life.

These earth-toned birds may appear dull from a distance, but if you are rewarded with a closer look, prepare to be awestruck by the beauty in their detail. Delicately striped, many appear the work of a master painter using a fine-tipped brush. Others are boldly patterned with patches of color and eye-catching contrasts. Short-necked and plump-bellied, sparrows move among their habitats readily, navigating with short hops.

The sparrow is the plant's best friend. These perky ground-dwellers are nature's seed spreaders. This is a perfect companionship, an efficient symbiosis, where everyone thrives.

Sparrows are underrated and sometimes overlooked, which is useful in survival, but we can miss them if we aren't looking and listening. Would this White-crowned Sparrow be easy to miss?

Exploring Ornitherapy

Put yourself into a day in the life of a sparrow... Force yourself to take a closer look. Intent in your focus, notice the details.

• How would you describe a sparrow?

• When still, what is its posture?

• Notice its bill. How does it use it?

• Watching its movements, are they easy to track?

• In your careful observations, can you predict what it will do next?

"Look at the sparrows; they do not know what they will do in the next moment. Let us literally live from moment to moment."
~ Mahatma Gandhi

Staying Afloat
39

Many birds use the surface of water as their "home-base" as life afloat offers them all they need to get by. Specially designed for buoyancy, light weight bone structures allow them to be carried on any type of water. Feathers structured like Velcro snap together to zipper-in air, creating an ideal innertube. This waterproofing beats any top-dollar slicker, insulating while doubling as designer wear.

Life on water requires a certain tenacity and fortitude in survival. Waterbirds are built to be seaworthy and resistant, remaining buoyant in the most turbulent conditions. They are unsinkable champions of the natural world.

We all have times in life when staying afloat can be a challenge. To find that buoyancy to keep us above water, birds can inspire us and give us the lift we need.

Exploring Ornitherapy

• Thinking about buoyancy, imagine yourself afloat. Would you rather be on the open sea, a river, or a small pond?

• When you see ducks like these Mallards, do they look happier in water or on land?

• If you have floated on water, did you enjoy it?

• Which water bird would you want to be, and why?

"Nothing is softer or more flexible than water, yet nothing can resist it."
~ Lao Tzu

Under the Surface: Feathered Divers and Fish-eaters
40

Just as some birds capture their prey on the wing, others "fly" under water's surface in pursuit of fishy meals. Predators who are piscivorous are obliged to a life around water, and skilled at making a living by eating fish.

Some are generalists and can eat a wide array of aquatic prey of all sizes. Others, like the Atlantic Puffin, are more specialized fishers of the sea, and require their meals to be precisely sized, especially when feeding young.

Like beach bums, birds are dressed for the part of the salt life. If you need to fly under the surface like this Atlantic Puffin, your body is likely adapted to the dynamics of underwater propulsion: a sleek, compact and muscular body, and short feathers, wings, and tail. Extreme divers of the avian world are equipped for the feat with higher blood volume, allowing them to store more oxygen for their deep journeys.

Perhaps you are a plunge-diver, gifted with keen eyesight, hovering above the surface eyeing food opportunities below. Terns, gannets, and Brown Pelicans, to name a few, excel at this style of precision fish-targeting.

Filling an ecological niche, these birds all play their part as consumers. With the fragility of our water ecosystems, their success depends upon a fine balance of all the links in our watersheds.

Exploring Ornitherapy

While we don't all live near water, we all live within a watershed, linked to distant habitats through these aquatic lifelines.

• Think about the bills of the fish-eaters you can name. Can you determine how they grab their prey by the shape of the bill they have?

• Have you ever been surprised by how big a fish a bird you were watching consumed? What adaptations must they have to do that?

• Have you ever watched a bird dive under water and return to the surface? Were you surprised by how long they stayed under? Could you do the same?

• If you could be a diving bird, which would it be?

"*Water is the driving force of all nature.*"
~ *Leonardo DaVinci*

Preening: An Avian Investment in the Future
41

Like all animals, birds need to take care of their bodies in order to optimize performance.

Adequate nutrition and exercise are key to longevity and survival, as well as tolerance to environmental factors such as climate and habitat. For birds, feather upkeep, called preening, is an integral part of the dynamics of life on the wing.

Feathers are critical equipment for a bird's survival. They are designed to last and perform. But like any valuable piece of hardware, they require routine maintenance for best preservation, and this is where the act of preening comes into play.

Birds are hard-wired to preen. The surface of a bird's body is covered in thousands of feathers. Each one plays a significant role in the bird's lifestyle and wellbeing; a collaborative, protective outerwear. Preening can be viewed as an investment in tomorrow for a bird, ensuring feather durability, cleanliness, and strength for survival. Bathing – in water or dust – lubricating with oil, or ruffling feathers are the most obvious behaviors we can notice.

Most birds are biologically outfitted with a specialized oil stored in the uropygial gland. Located on the upperparts of the bird's body, it lies beneath the skin and is fixed at the base of the tail. The preening oil is thought to be chemically constructed to enable waterproofing, antibacterial defenses, feather brightening, and general feather health and cleanliness - much like shampoo. It is thought that the oil contains a personalized signature stamp to attract mates and possibly defend territory.

Studies on bird behavior show that most birds spend 8-10% of their day on preening behaviors. If we watch birds long enough, we might see them carefully rearranging feathers, oiling, bathing, or dusting. This Sandhill Crane was easy to watch as it methodically preened in the sun.

"Love the world as your own self, then you can truly care for all things."
~ Lao Tzu

Exploring Ornitherapy

While watching birds outside your door:

• Can you find preening or self-care behavior?

• How long did the preening last?

• Which preening behavior do you observe most often?

• Would you describe the preening behaviors to be methodical and patterned, or carefree and spontaneous?

• If you observe a bird bathing in water, how does it behave? Does it seem alert and watchful, or relaxed and comfortable?

• Are you able to see a noticeable difference in the way a bird looks after it has preened?

• Do you take time daily for your own self care?

Journal (page 192)

The Bug Life
42

Insects are abundant around us. You don't have to look far outside your door to find them. They are the most diverse set of organisms on the planet. While they can be seen as a nuisance to humans in many ways, they are critical to our own survival, and that of the ecosystem surrounding us. Some are hard to live with, but we cannot live without them and neither can the birds.

Bugs – insects and other multi-legged invertebrates – provide essential nutrients for birds and other wildlife. Nature sustains bug life through the plant diversity they require as host foods in their specialized habitats. The relationship between insects and plants is fundamental and powerful. Plants are the motherboard of insect life, and the niche each species fills is critical within their required habitat. Sometimes insects thrive as parasites, getting nourishment from the blood of other animals (as this Willow Ptarmigan can attest to).

A bird's life cycle booms in concert with its food sources. We enjoy feeding birds in our yards and gardens, but nature is the ultimate bird feeder. Trees, shrubs, and other plant life abound with bug life, many too small for us to notice. If you have plants which naturally occur, the insects and birds will come.

Life outdoors is busy for most animals. Birds thrive off readily available insects, especially during the nesting season when high proteins are paramount to offspring survival. Some birds are observant of human disturbance of bug life, and benefit from the way in which we manage crops and landscapes. Other populations plummet due to our disruption of the ecological systems around us. Birds can flourish in our wake, and provide us healthier environments as a result by keeping the bug life in check.

"If all mankind were to disappear, the world would regenerate back to the rich state of equilibrium that existed ten thousand years ago. If insects were to vanish, the environment would collapse into chaos."
~ E. O. Wilson

Exploring Ornitherapy

• Have you noticed birds outside your door dining on insect life?

• Which feeding behavior is most noticeable: birds that eat while on the wing, or those who pick and glean off plants?

• If you see a bird with a bug in its mouth, can you identify the bug?

• Have you ever noticed swallows chasing machinery?

• Can we live without insects?

Journal (page 193)

Bird Feet

43

There's an old saying, "Don't' judge a book by its cover." But can you judge a bird by its feet? Equipped with multiple adaptations, a bird's feet are more than just useful appendages.

Uniquely specialized to their environments, bird feet differ greatly from species to species. Scaly, webbed, or clawed, a bird's feet are essential tools to navigating through life.

Fancy footwear is adapted to straddling vegetation in water, for scaling trees, perching, propelling through water, and sometimes seizing prey. The size and shape of the feet keep a bird in business, offering protection, locomotion, and in the case of the raptor, the power to capture prey. This Snail Kite's talons nearly match the shape of its bill – do you know why?

If we look closely, we can learn a lot about a bird by paying attention to how it uses its feet, and which habitat it best thrives in.

Exploring Ornitherapy

• Can you find examples of differently shaped feet on the birds in your neighborhood?

• Compare the feet of at least two species and see if you can notice differences. Why might they be different? What advantages do feet give a particular species?

• Have you noticed how the birds around you use their feet?

• Do you ever watch a woodpecker's feet as it climbs up a tree?

• Which feet intrigue you the most?

• If you could have a pair of bird's feet to use, which would you pick?

"*Walk as if you are kissing the earth beneath your feet.*"
~ *Thich Nhat Hanh*

Journal (page 194)

Camouflage
44

For many animals, camouflage is an essential device for living and survival. It is both the trickery used by predators, and the obscurity which services prey. We don't have to look far outside our own door to see where an animal or bird uses this disguise to their own advantage in survival.

Birds are masters in the art of concealment. For many species, their bodies biologically dictate feather molt, the process where feathers are replaced to pivot a bird's advantage of survival by blending into a seasonal habitat. Muted winter colors of the American Goldfinch, for example, are not just a fashion statement in concert with winter's duller tones. These seasonal changes are effective as a tool of evasion from predators when it's harder to hide while feeding in barren trees or fields.

Predatory birds, like bitterns, can stalk their prey because their color patterns mimic their habitat: tall, long reeds. These masters of disguise also use their posture for the ultimate fooling – pointing their bills to the sky while swaying their bodies back and forth as if blowing in the wind – a graceful dance of mimicry.

The Brown Creeper is a cryptic wizard, its body blending into the wallpaper of tree bark, only noticeable with intense observation or the hint of movement revealing its presence.

Owls and nightjars like this Common Pauraque, and other birds most active amid darkness, are patterned to be obscured among their habitats. They blend in so well they avoid disturbance by day and are hidden from their prey.

Examples of camouflage can be obvious or difficult to pick out. All are advantages for the everyday art of survival.

Exploring Ornitherapy

• Looking at the birds around you, can you find examples of camouflaged feather patterns?

• Which bird in your neighborhood is best at the art of camouflage?

• Have you ever been surprised or startled by a well-camouflaged bird?

• Do you ever find yourself using the art of camouflage?

"Happiness is seeing blessings in disguise, beauty under camouflage, and love amid conflict."
~ Richelle E. Goodrich

Variability in Birds and Life
45

In life, variability is found everywhere and in everything. In nature, variability is abundant, even if subtle and not obvious. Sometimes we just need to look harder to find it.

With birds, this is no different. Individual birds are incredibly variable, just like people. While our expectations of a bird are shaped by the prototype specimen of a single species – like what we might find in some field guides– each individual is uniquely different in many ways. But do we automatically see these differences when we look? If we spend time observing and getting to know the birds around us, we learn these differences – just like we get to know and learn the personalities of our friends.

When we focus on listening to birds sing, we often discover that their songs are variable and unique to individuals. The way they sound is influenced by their geography. Like people, some birds have regional dialects that we can hear. Individual birds will sing their own songs. Whether we can detect these variances or not, they exist. The same is true of color, and lightness versus darkness, which can also impact where and how a bird lives.

Can birds dictate their own individuality? Are they able to control their own appearance, or how they sound? These are questions that have no conclusive answers, but when we recognize the fact that birds react to their own environments just as we do, the answer seems clear that birds are capable of individuality in ways we cannot appreciate. Nature versus nurture is the age-old debate, especially when we examine ourselves as animals. Birds are just as impacted by the same influences. Their survivability depends on these effects in many ways.

Birds are individuals. They are all different and shaped by the world around them, just like we are.

Exploring Ornitherapy

• Is it easy to pick out variabilities in birds of the same species? Do you see this in color patterns? Color tones? Look at the many variations of these House Finches. If we look closely each one is different from the next.

• Can you hear variability in the songs of an individual bird? For example, if you have Song Sparrows in your yard, do they all sing the exact same song? What other bird songs are similar, yet not quite the same?

• Are you able to notice any differences in behaviors of the individuals of the same species? If you get to know them well enough, can you pick out the same bird in your neighborhood?

• Do you find it hard to notice variances in individual birds, and if so, is that because of your own expectations of what you anticipate seeing, or because the differences are subtle and hard to detect?

"Never think that lack of variability is stability."
~ Nassim Taleb

Journal (page 196)

Avian Athletes: Migration Miracles
46

As you read this, somewhere in the world bird migration is underway... Avian migration is undeniably one of the most fascinating marvels and incredible feats of movement known on planet earth.

Birds are superstar athletes: marathon sky-runners. Some accomplish feats of self-powered distance in a single year unparalleled in the animal world. Known to be capable of covering more than 44,000 miles in a calendar year, the World Distance Champion Arctic Tern pictured here circumnavigates the globe, pole to pole, continent to continent. This is mind-blowing, when put into context that this same tern will return to the same rock to nest on, decade after decade.

With the aid of navigation tracking devices, researchers were able to crown the Bar-tailed Godwit the Longest Distance Nonstop Traveler award. No layovers for this intrepid flier. From Alaska to New Zealand, a female Bar-tailed Godwit flew 7,250 miles in an eight-day journey with no rest, food, or water. And this was not a one-time event. This is just a chapter in the lifecycle of long-distance fliers – what this bird, and others like her, are built to do, year after year.

It's estimated that 5 billion birds globally migrate each year, representing 40% of all bird species. Poising yourself in the right place and time, you can catch a glimpse of migration in action. A spectator's sport, visible migration is just as thrilling to witness as performances of athleticism of any human match or ballgame.

We can optimize our encounters with migratory birds by watching weather patterns and understanding the timing of migration for the species we are most interested in finding. Migratory birds depend on tail winds to propel them forward. Storms can impede the journey, but also provide an assist in launching a single bird skyward with frequent flier miles.

Migrating birds can appear anywhere. We can catch glimpses of these feathered premier leaguers as they stop over in our neighborhoods, packing on the fat to fuel the next leg of their journeys. Migration is timed in concert with the availability of a reliable food source to power these athletes onward, but only if the fragile balance of nature is not disrupted.

Birds are incredible, and migration is awe inspiring. Nature is powerful.

"It's good to have an end in mind, but in the end what counts is how you travel."
~ Orna Ross

Exploring Ornitherapy

• Have you noticed migrant birds on the wing, heading to destinations hundreds or thousands of miles away?

• Have you seen birds using your neighborhood as a pit stop, actively feeding and refueling before jetting off to faraway places? Do you know what they were eating while visiting?

• Do you have a favorite migrant bird that you seek out during a leg of its journey? If so, why is it your favorite – how it looks, sounds, or it's athleticism?

• What's your favorite mystery of migration?

• Do you consider yourself to "migrate" anywhere?

Journal (page 197)

The Bird's Eye View: Birds View Us
47

We spend so much time hoping to get closer looks at birds, to see them better and understand who they are. Closer proximity, whether through glass or with our own eyes, allows for a style of voyeurism – a peek into the lives of another animal. Do you think the tables are ever turned? Do birds watch us, and anticipate our behaviors or actions? Do they get to know us as individuals?

It's clear through research that some birds are able to recognize individual humans and associate them with different behaviors. Birds in the corvid family, like crows and magpies, can learn the people around them and watch them for behavioral clues. Other species that cohabitate among people, like mockingbirds, and pigeons, have been known to use facial recognition. If birds can recognize us, is this an advantage for their survival?

If we know that birds, or even other animals, are watching us, does it make us think about how we behave and interact with the world around us?

If we set up a sit-spot in our yards, gardens, or even the local park, we can become familiar to the birds living around us. The longer and more continually we sit, the more familiar the birds become. They begin to anticipate our behaviors and learn that we are not a threat.

To do this, position a chair in a spot that will not move. Place it close to where birds are active. Then strategize familiarity by always wearing the same clothing and hat while in your sit-spot. This is important, and enables birds get used to what they are seeing. Dedicate time to sit as still and quietly as possible. The more time you spend here, the quicker the birds will adapt to you. Eventually, they will acclimate to you, and allow for a more intimate experience of observation.

"The most beautiful gift of nature is that it gives one pleasure to look around and try to comprehend what we see."
~ Albert Einstein

• Have you noticed birds outside your door tuned into your behaviors, routines, or actions? The Tufted Titmouse often appears curious and watchful, especially around bird feeders needing a refill!

• Do you think there are birds that recognize you?

• Do birds in your neighborhood take advantage of human actions, or impact on habitats?

• Which birds seem the most easily disturbed, or flushed, by people?

• Have you noticed some birds in your neighborhood are less wary of you?

Journal (page 198)

Mob Rules: A Call to Attention
48

You don't need to be fluent in birdsong or calls to understand and interpret the alarms ringing out in the bird world. Fine-tuning your ears for the pulsating and angry calls might lead you to a discovery easily gone unnoticed and offer you a glimpse into an action-packed world of a dynamic food chain.

Like the town criers, birds like crows, jays, chickadees, and titmice are some of the alarmists that keep everyone apprised of predatory threats in your neighborhood. When a jay spies a hawk sitting undercover, it moves in closer and begins sounding the alarm as if screaming, "I gotcha! You're out," shining a glaring light on the Cooper's Hawk silently stalking the birds at your feeder. Soon other birds begin appearing on the scene, and the cast of feathered characters in your yard emerges on stage as everyone comes in to investigate. This is a great way to learn and study birds. Watch who is bold and who stays in the background, peeking out behind the brush yet still curious.

During the nesting season, if you pay attention to airborne birds you might witness dive-bombing behavior as a smaller bird swoops down on a larger one – whether perched or in the air. In this photo, the jaeger dives at the biologist as she walks near the nest site, a tactic of protection.

Turkey Vultures, Red-tailed Hawks, and other birds are often the targets of this fearless tactic attempting to force the avian threat out of the airspace.

Look for birds with an eye turned skyward and find their target. Birds are the ultimate hawkwatchers, their intent gaze reveals the Peregrine Falcon over your head. Becoming aware of our world through the eyes of birds, we can learn a lot about ourselves and other animals.

"In order to see birds, it is necessary to become part of the silence."
~ Robert Lynd

Exploring Ornitherapy

• Have you ever become aware of angry or scolding calls of birds in your yard?

• Were you ever the subject of mobbing behavior by birds in your yard?

• Have you ever found a hawk or an owl thanks to a mob of birds calling it out?

• Would this sort of mobbing behavior of known threats work within a human social structure?

• Is it already in use anywhere in our own society?

Journal (page 199)

Bothersome Birds
49

It's never hard to pick out the birds we have a fondness for. But is there a bird that you don't like, or get frustrated by? Bird behaviors can sometimes be off-putting to us. We find fault in their actions even when we invited them in – historically, or as guests of our gardens.

It's easy to have unfavorable opinions of birds who weren't always a natural part of the local ecosystem but have adapted brilliantly to thrive. Often these introduced species are able to out-compete the native birds, forcing them out of their nesting cavities, optimizing their own nesting success. When we think about natural history, we learn that these birds are only doing what they are programmed to do, much like any of us in the animal world: survive and thrive. We assisted in their promotion, so are they really to blame?

Sometimes it's gregarious behavior that earns a bird a bad reputation. Birds that flock to our feeders in throngs, sweeping out the seeds, dominating the scene can be off-putting, and even expensive!

Other times we are annoyed by predatory behaviors we encounter, such as a bird's savvy skills at predation, nest-robbing, or nest-parasitism. While we love to feed birds in our yards, we must keep in mind that we are essentially offering a birdfeeder to the avian apex predators, who will equally benefit from the buffets.

When we think about the birds we do not like, we need to ask ourselves why. As a conservation piece, it's important to remember that thinking more about why will lead to a better understanding of ecological roles. For example, raptors were once thought of as pests. But, in taking a closer look at their role in the ecosystem, we see the incredible value they have. Discussions on relationships between people and birds are important in order to further stewardship and understanding.

Exploring Ornitherapy

• Can you think of a bird that you do not like?

• When we don't like a particular bird, is it because of the way they impact people and landscapes, or is it their behavior with other birds that is bothersome?

• The birds on the horse's back are in fact helping it by picking off bugs, but these Brown-headed Cowbirds are deemed a pest for behaviors of nest parasitism. So are they always "bad birds," or are they actually good?

• Imagine these same identifiable negative behaviors, and ask yourself: if these were people, would I admire these behaviors?

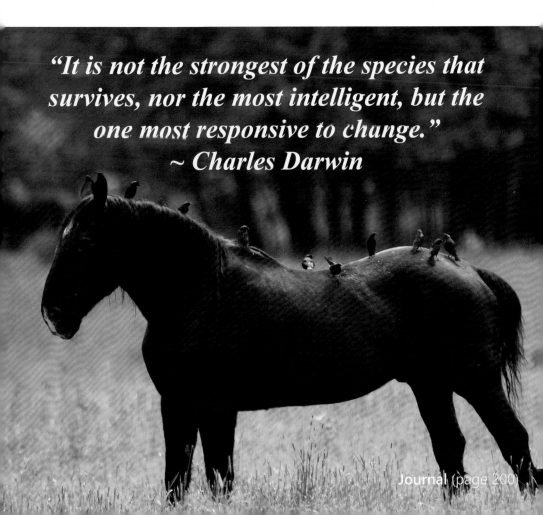

"It is not the strongest of the species that survives, nor the most intelligent, but the one most responsive to change."
~ Charles Darwin

Journal (page 200)

Meditation 4: Visualizing Connection

Although we might be individual beings, we are deeply connected to the world around us. We are connected biologically to our families, emotionally to our friends, and physically to our environment.

When was the last time you thought about how many connections you have in this world?

Exploring Mindfulness

Close your eyes and start to focus on the present moment.

Think about the emotional and biological connections that are present in your life. Visualize who they are and what these relationships look like:
- Parents, siblings, children
- Significant others
- Friends
- Pets (yes, that's still a connection!)

Beyond emotional connections, think about your environmental connections:
• How are we connected to the earth?
• How are we connected to the birds and animals around us?
• How do we interact with birds daily?
• What impact do we have on the lives of birds around us?
• What impacts do birds and animals have on our lives?

Notice your physical connections:
• What are you touching right now?
• Are your feet touching the earth, flooring inside your house, or a sock or shoe that you are wearing?
• What does it feel like to touch the bark on a tree, or soil on the ground?

It is easy to lose track of the connections we have to the world around us when we are distracted. Remember to take time every day and bring awareness and appreciation to these connections – they are so important in our lives!

"The most beautiful gift of nature is that it gives one pleasure to look around and try to comprehend what we see."
~Albert Einstein

Nest Cavities: Hope for New Beginnings
50

Spring unfolds after winter's rest, and life renews and emerges. Loud orchestras of birdsong, eruptions of bright colors, and promise of new life resound. Birds are getting busy. Approaching the nesting time, birdsong heralds the new season as birds begin to seek prime real estate to raise young – ensuring continued survival of their kind.

Nesting strategies differ from species to species. Many birds across the globe are dependent upon shelters called cavities for nesting, roosting, and evading predators. Cavity nesting enables some of our songbirds to nest earlier than others due to the natural amenities and securities. Some birds, like woodpeckers, are skilled excavators, and chisel out a perfectly customized hideaway. Many birds aren't equipped with built-in carpentry tools. Instead, they use the old construction of other birds, or even insects like termites.

With human-directed changes in landscapes and habitats, cavities are precious real estate in the natural world. Structures sufficient for nesting are dwindling. But there's some hope, if we start to recognize habitat requirements and assist nature's lost opportunities. We can support birds that require cavities in many ways. A win-win for birds and people is offering cavities like boxes, or allowing dead trees to remain standing and take on new life. As a sort of landlord, we assume the role of stewards for the next nest generation. The benefits of these simple acts will reverberate within us and in the natural landscapes surrounding us.

It is good to recognize that we can make a difference. Species we adore, like bluebirds and Wood Ducks, were saved through conservation efforts, including implementing nest boxes. The declining American Kestrel, Purple Martins, and Chimney Swifts could benefit if similar conservation practices with nesting cavities were put into place.

Bringing bird life closer brings a measure of joy. But even if we aren't able to offer suitable homes in our own gardens, we can find cavities outside our doors if we spend time looking.

Exploring Ornitherapy

• Look around. Can you find hollows or spaces that would be suitable for nesting?

• How many cavity nesting species can you find in your neighborhood?

• Listen for drumming on wood. Can you detect woodpeckers around you?

• If you have a nest box nearby, is anyone using it?

"Spring work is going on with joyful enthusiasm."
~ John Muir

Aerial Insectivores: Dining on the Wing
51

Watching the acrobatic air dance of birds eating insects on the wing is not only entertaining but mesmerizing. Swooping and swirling in the air, their movements illuminate the paths of invisible insects that they pursue. Quick-turn maneuvers and speed are feats of aerodynamics that impress even the most skilled fighter pilots.

Superstars of air agility, they work endlessly consuming massive amounts of insects that make up layers in the airspace above and around us. Some, like swallows, are generalists, and go where the insects are, flying so high that they stretch the limits of altitude. Others, like some flycatchers, sit perched, and watch and wait for the perfect meal. They sail through the air before launching airborne – an "out and back" approach, known as sallying or hawking. Some raptors, like kites, snatch insects from the sky for a quick airborne snack.

Nature's job assignment of the avian aerial insectivores, which include the nightjars (nighthawks, whip-poor-wills, etc.), swifts, swallows, martins and flycatchers, and some hawks like this Mississippi Kite, is to help keep the insect mass on the planet in balance.

As you look to the skies when they are around, allow them to carry your eyes on their wings. Watch how they work. Bring to your mind a sense of freedom and peace by their graceful movements and confident agility. Know that they are doing their part to help the greater good of our shared world. Be inspired by them to do yours.

"No bird soars too high if he soars with his own wings."
~ William Blake

Exploring Ornitherapy

Challenge yourself to find insect-eating birds and take note of how they are designed and built.

Shape and Aerodynamics:

• Take note of the wings and the tail.

• What stands out with the shape of the wings?

• Is the tail long or short?

• Is the tail forked or notched?

• Does the overall shape make sense to how the bird needs to maneuver and feed?

• Does the shape assist with speed?

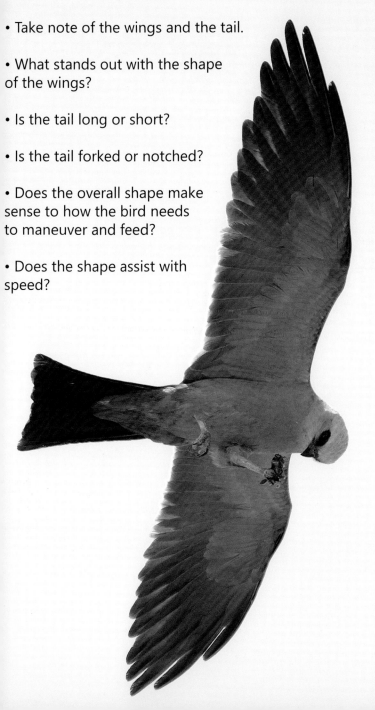

Journal (page 203)

Wading Birds
52

Head turners, Great Blue Herons and other tall waders command our attention: still as a statue, on two legs, and upright, just like us. Graceful, yet stealthy, wading birds are charismatic in every sense of the word.

The wading birds include herons, egrets, flamingos, ibis, storks, and spoonbills, to name a few. A lifestyle with a water's view, they can be found in wet habitats across the globe. Highly adaptive, they source food in even the tiniest of wetlands.

Many are solo hunters, but value congregation. There's community in their nesting sites. Where there's one there can be many. Waders also flock together at night to roost in trees, adorning the boughs like living ornaments on a Christmas tree.

Their striking features may appear awkward: large bodies stacked onto long, thin legs and long, thin necks bolstering small heads with long specially-designed bills. These birds exemplify some of the best animal adaptations.

Big and easy to watch as they work, the waders demonstrate skill and perfection of their sport. Exhibiting work ethics of patience and precision, waders are the envy of every good fishermen.

Exploring Ornitherapy

• Which words would you use to describe a wading bird's feeding technique?

• Pick a wader and assign one word to describe its feeding style.

• Thinking about the personalities and feeding behaviors of wading birds, which one would be closest to your own? Quiet, still, and statuesque like a Great Blue Heron? Perhaps filled with spunk and drama, like the Reddish Egret? Moving along methodically and gracefully like a flamingo? There are many to choose from...

"Advice from a Great Blue Heron:
Wade into life.
Keep a keen lookout.
Don't be afraid to get your feet wet.
Be patient.
Look below the surface.
Enjoy a good reed.
Go fish!"
~ Ilan Shamir

Journal (page 204)

Scavengers
53

We don't have to look far into the natural world to find a feathered ally who helps curtail the spread of diseases and harmful bacteria: the vultures. These scavengers undertake the role of devouring recently dead animals, often leaving only the skeletal frame behind. Largely underappreciated due to their ominous reputation and naked heads, vultures are some of our most effective waste managers. Without their gutsy work ethic in servicing our communities, diseases and bacteria would advance the frontlines and challenge the health of nearby habitats, including our own. Adapted with powerful acids in their digestive tract, consumed bacteria is all but exterminated. And while they are on the job, self-protective measures may include their own excrement. Vultures urinate on their legs while standing on the decaying flesh, and their uric acid is thought to be the ultimate sanitizer keeping germs at bay. Heads lacking feathers, a feature we tend to find unsightly, is another natural success in hygiene upkeep - preventing bacteria from festering on would-be feathers after exploring messy carcasses.

Vultures are arguably the MVPs of the bird world. Skilled team players, they work together in the airspace while finding their next feast. Cleaning up roadkill casualties, they can be seen huddled in curbside parties while performing their "dirty work." Social animals, vultures group together in large roosts for night using tall spruces or other structures as their communal rest areas.

Superb fliers, these long-winged birds supremely navigate thermal columns and wind currents in the most careful and deliberate way in order to stay aloft without flapping. They are the ultimate energy savers of flight. Unlocking all the secrets in the airspace, they are masters of the sky.

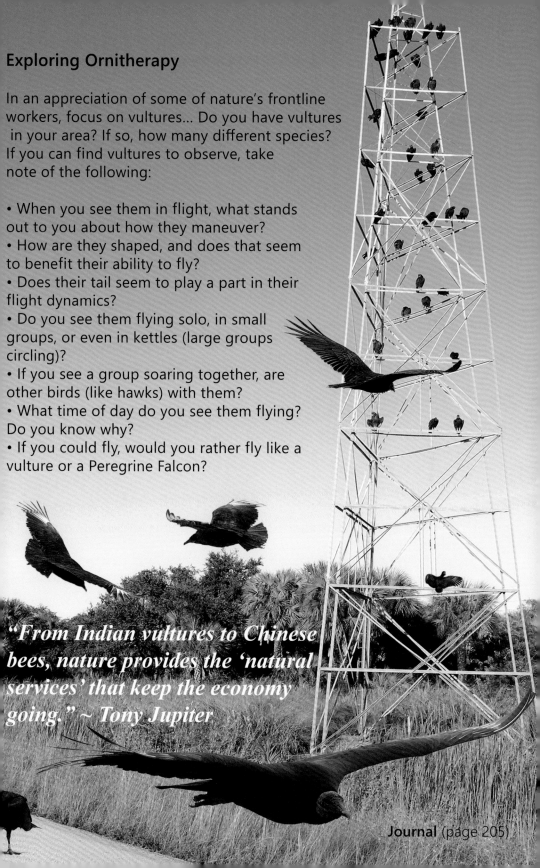

Exploring Ornitherapy

In an appreciation of some of nature's frontline
workers, focus on vultures... Do you have vultures
in your area? If so, how many different species?
If you can find vultures to observe, take
note of the following:

• When you see them in flight, what stands
out to you about how they maneuver?
• How are they shaped, and does that seem
to benefit their ability to fly?
• Does their tail seem to play a part in their
flight dynamics?
• Do you see them flying solo, in small
groups, or even in kettles (large groups
circling)?
• If you see a group soaring together, are
other birds (like hawks) with them?
• What time of day do you see them flying?
Do you know why?
• If you could fly, would you rather fly like a
vulture or a Peregrine Falcon?

*"From Indian vultures to Chinese
bees, nature provides the 'natural
services' that keep the economy
going." ~ Tony Jupiter*

Apex Predators
54

Watching a bird of prey in flight, or in active pursuit of prey, can be thrilling. These magnificent birds are both fierce and beautiful. They captivate our attention. If we are lucky enough to find one nearby to watch, they inspire awe and intrigue.

Are we as humans impressed by them because of their capabilities of speed? Or because many have binocular vision like we do? Or is it that we innately know they keep balance in our shared environment?

Birds of prey sit at the top of the food chain. They are apex predators of the avian world. They balance populations of their prey, and nature needs balance to thrive. Without it the system slips out of line. We share the same ecosystem and food chain. We suffer without these integral parts of the web working in harmony. Birds of prey are champions in our ecosystem.

Exploring Ornitherapy

• Name an avian apex predator in your neighborhood – it can be diurnal, crepuscular, or nocturnal.

• Think of one way they are beneficial in your neighborhood.

• If you can't find one in your neighborhood, which one would you appoint to take on a shift and why?

• Which bird of prey do you most admire, and why?

"*Let nature be your teacher.*"
~ *William Wordsworth*

Celebrating Roles
55

Not all birds are visually separable by sex to the human eye, but some males and females are easy to tell apart. Most female birds tend to be less colorful or less brightly patterned, a clever adaptation for survival. Often this camouflaging helps hide her while tending a nest or young.

Males tend to be more colorful to our eyes, and often boldly patterned. Male songbirds, who typically have the role of claiming territory, advertise themselves through bold melodies or vocalizations. Other male birds, like ducks or grebes, offer elaborate performances, or dances, choreographed to impress females enough to mate.

In some cases, like the Red-necked Phalarope (and all phalaropes), the color roles reverse and the females are more colorful. That's because the females lay their eggs and the males do the rest of the job of rearing the young, from incubating onward. Meanwhile, the females seek other males to produce more eggs. The scientific term for this is polyandry.

Roles birds play are critical to the survival of the species. Nature is dependent on the differentiation of the sexes. Watching for clues of behavior, song, or even patterns of color offer us a glimpse into the lifestyles and fascinating worlds of birds.

Exploring Ornitherapy

• Can you identify the females or the males of any bird species? Do any of them jump out at you as obvious?

• If you cannot determine the sex visually, can you find behavioral clues that may give it away?

• Have you watched a female building a nest or tending to young? Was she doing this alone or with her mate? Could you tell if the bird building the nest was male or female?

• What is your favorite behavior that is specific to either a male or female bird?

"Mother nature has the power to please, to comfort, to calm, and to power one's soul."
~ Anthony Douglas Williams

Journal (page 207)

Celebrating Roles II
56

When the nesting season is underway, it is interesting to note the roles male and female birds play (or don't play) in the process of nesting, incubating, and tending to their young. While the females are always the egg layers, studying nesting birds closely reveals some dedicated fathers who are solely responsible for the upbringing and survival of their clutches.

Avian contestants for "Dad of the Year" would most definitely include those in the shorebird family. These male birds stand out in their attentive chick rearing and efforts to raise the next generation.

The male Willets are the "night-shifters" – they incubate their clutches of eggs through the night while the females are mostly (but not exclusively) the day-sitters. After hatching, the females abandon the chicks entirely after just two weeks, leaving the males behind to brood the chicks for another couple of weeks until fledging.

Short-billed Dowitcher males play a similar role. They split the duties of incubation with their mates, but when the chicks hatch nearly all parental care is done by the male. He tends to the chicks until they fledge, while the females leave the scene and begin migrating south. He stays on with the chicks for weeks after her departure, ensuring the survival and fledging of the clutch.

Male Wilson's Phalaropes (and other phalaropes) are likely the winners of the prize, and avian Superstar Dads: The female Wilson's Phalarope deserts the male after she lays the clutch of eggs. The male does all the rest – from incubation, to feeding until fledging – with the female nowhere in sight. In fact, a single female may lay multiple clutches with multiple males...then skip town leaving the guys in it for the long haul. This phenomenon in biology is called polyandry.

If we pay enough attention to the lives of the birds around us, we will quickly discover the incredible lifestyles and sagas underway. This isn't much different than a modern-day soap opera!

"The heart of a father is the masterpiece of nature."
~ Antoine Francois Prevost

Exploring Ornitherapy

• When observing birds during the nesting season, have you noticed roles of male and female birds?

• Have you noticed which sex bird is gathering or carrying food to a nest? Are there more females or males working to feed their young?

• Which of the sexes is carrying nesting material or doing the nest building?

• If you see a family of birds together, are you able to discern the sex of the parents by behavior if the color patterns are the same in both adults?

• Do you have a favorite male bird?

Patterns of Color
57

In nature we can find patterns reverberating everywhere. Patterns in birds are abundant: in how a bird looks, behaves, and what it sounds like. Symmetry, fractals, spirals, tessellations, rhythms, and more: patterns in nature and birds are not accidental.

Birds exhibit flashy examples of patterns of color. These patterns engage us, jumping out to our eyes. We're instinctively attracted to them; they draw us in.

Some patterns are hard to ignore on birds. Others are subtle and we have to look hard to find them. Their arrangement can form intricate designs. Patterns of color on birds serve purpose: camouflaging, attraction, foiling predators, and interspecies recognition.

Patterns of color are also excellent clues in the identification of birds; they can be very consistent in a bird's life. When combined with size, shape, behavior, and habitat, identifying bird becomes much easier. Despite its large size, this Great Horned Owl can hide very easily due to its patterns.

Exploring Ornitherapy

Focus on patterns of color on the birds outside your door.

• Which of these patterns really grab your attention?

• Do those patterns have high contrast, light to dark?

• Are they eye catching all the time, or only while the bird is in flight?

• On which part of the bird's anatomy (face, wings, tail, etc.) do you think it's easiest to spot a pattern of color?

• Does the pattern set this species apart from other birds around it?

• Focus on the boldest patterns on a bird you can find. See if you can figure out why these patterns would be an advantage, or disadvantage, to the bird.

"*There is no better designer than nature.*"
~ *Alexander McQueen*

Connecting Others to Birds
58

Challenge yourself to think of someone to reach out to who may not already be looking outdoors to find peace or joy, but would benefit from what you can show them.

Sharing experiences in nature and with birds, even digitally, can be incredibly powerful for another person.

How can you brighten someone's day by connecting them to birds or nature?

Exploring Ornitherapy

How did they react and how did it make you feel?

What did you learn from teaching someone how to connect to birds or nature?

Was there a highlight for you in this experience?

Go make someone's day.

"The heart that gives, gathers."
~The Tao Te Ching

Journal (page 210)

Meditation 5: Cultivating Curiousity

Children are notorious for asking the most difficult questions with only one word: why? Why don't dinosaurs exist anymore? Why can't penguins fly? Why is the sky blue?

It seems that as we grow older, society drains this curiosity from our minds. With Ornitherapy, we seek to rejuvenate this desire to learn, in conjunction with birds and nature. Start asking more questions and wondering why the world works the way it does. Look at nature and life with a new perspective. Let this perspective guide you through the present moment.

Exploring Mindfulness

Find a comfortable seat outside. Start to let go of the day thus far and focus on your breath. Release any tension or stress you are carrying and focus on being here.

Begin to think about the environment and world around you. Notice the presence of other magnificent life forms that are present: birds, other animals, people. Let your mind open to one feeling: curiosity.

Let the energy and feeling that comes along with curiosity expand throughout your mind and body. Feel curious about your breath, the way the air feels around you, the sounds of nature you hear.

Explore physical sensations with curiosity.
• How does your body feel right now?
• What comes to your attention?
• How do you feel in your current environment, and why do you think you feel this way?
•Think of questions to ask yourself!

Have fun noticing these sensations. Greet them with kindness and waive judgement.

Everyone will experience curiosity differently. We all have unique interests, and therefore notice individual details that are personal to us.

"*The future belongs
to the curious.*"
~ *Anonymous*

How Birds Saved My Life
By Holly

Birds are medicine for the mind, body, and soul...

Here is photo of me birding in the White Mountains of New Hampshire, halfway through a six-month rigorous course of chemotherapy for breast cancer. Baldness hidden by a wig, I'm wearing a beaming smile, because being in nature and watching birds was what nourished my spirit and gave me strength and courage to summit a different kind of mountain.

Connecting to birds and nature was a front-line weapon in my battle. And, for me it was as powerful as the conventional treatments enlisted to restore my health. Birding brought me peace, mental recharging, and restoration of energy in ways I cannot describe.

As all-consuming a cancer diagnosis can be, I didn't allow this game changer to steal me from my love of birds and birding. Birding while undergoing treatment set me on a path towards healing and recovery, and into a metamorphosis of my "new normal."

The respite Ornitherapy provides from the chronic grip of crisis can be likened to opening a door into a temporary world of peace. My focus while birding shifted from my own survival to the survival of birds and the pressures they face. I lost my hair from chemo on Mother's Day eve. The next morning, I went out to search for birds and process this loss. I remember being completely in the moment of observation when I serendipitously found the nest of Cerulean Warblers - a species rare in my area. The experience of watching another young family in survival mode, put a lot into perspective for me as I worked through my own will to live.

To bring the birds closer at a time when I couldn't easily move around, I saved all the hair I lost from the effects of chemo and placed it in a suet cage to offer as nesting material for the birds to gather that spring. The satisfaction of watching a Tufted Titmouse pull strands of my wasted hair, and carry it away, made the personal loss purposeful. And emphasized that simple things can be so powerful.

During tough times in life, we all need to find what fills us up and helps us recharge. We can then find fortitude and peace amidst the storms. Birds are my go-to therapy and medicine. I hope they will be yours, too.

Finding Common Ground
By Richard

I don't have a favorite bird but I do love the Sanderling for what we have in common. Sanderlings are sturdily built and always on the run, being chased out of the ocean by the waves. They travel all over the world and wear so many different colors depending on what they are doing.

Clearly, there are similarities in our lifestyles. But am I a birder, photographer, a researcher, a conservationist, or something else? None of them, all of them? I don't know! I suppose they are all just tools or excuses for me to be connected with nature. I am an animal and I love being in nature where animals belong. I need to be in it; I feel that. It makes me healthier, happier and it is who I am.

My Breathless Blue Therapy
By Sophie

I was one of the first generations to grow up entirely surrounded by technology. It's easy to see how the importance of nature can get lost in the noise of cell phones, social media, and the ever-important "like." Luckily, I grew up in a household that emphasized the value of time spent outdoors, where the air is fresh and pixelated screens are far away.

While traveling the world in 2019, I stumbled across a sport called freediving that allowed me to seamlessly integrate my love for nature with mindfulness. Mindfulness is a term that has been trending over the past few years and may be familiar to some. Simply put, mindfulness is the act of bringing awareness to the present moment without judgement.

While lesser known but certainly growing in popularity, freediving is highly intertwined with mindfulness. In simple terms, freediving is swimming to depth while holding your breath without any breathing apparatuses. Anyone can do it! Whenever you hold you breath and swim down, you are technically freediving.

Appreciating and experiencing nature is a cornerstone of my identity, and freediving allows me to not only explore the environment around me, but also myself. When I dip beneath the surface and the water silences the chaos of the world above, I escape into the ocean and into myself. It is a tranquility I have never experienced anywhere else on this planet.

Away from the noise beyond the shore, freediving is a time for me to check in with my body and mind. How am I feeling? What parts of my body are carrying tension? Am I focusing on the present moment, or is my mind somewhere above the surface?

The awareness I experience while I dive is something I strive to carry with me throughout the day. I focus on being mindful towards myself, but also of the environment around me. What do I see? How am I interacting with other people, with the world around me? When we learn about the environment, birds, and other wildlife, we also learn about ourselves.

As humans, we have a default tendency to focus on "me, myself, and I," but with mindfulness we can expand an awareness of ourself to the world around us, and with freediving we can integrate that awareness with respect and appreciation for the natural world.

OBJECTS IN MIRROR ARE
CLOSER THAN THEY APPEAR

Journaling: Taking Note

When we dial into the natural world, we become instantly connected to life around us. Our minds start conversing with our ears and eyes translating our experiences into observations. These observations allow us to build knowledge and understanding, benefitting us many ways. In the field, we often use equipment like binoculars, spotting scopes, and cameras to support our vision. The field journal, or notebook, is a tool to support our minds. This tool can be as valuable as the optics we carry as we become better observers.

The act of translating what your senses perceive onto paper is cognitively beneficial. It requires heightened attention and concentration. By transcribing through words or imagery, you are enlisting your senses to examine and ask questions in new ways. Journaling also enlists both sides of the brain: the analytical left and the creative right. This dual hemispheric engagement enhances your focus in a cathartic way.

There are also proven health benefits to journaling, which is why we feel it's the perfect compliment to Ornitherapy. Journaling has been found to improve overall wellbeing. It can boost your mood, provide clarity in your thought process, and improve your memory.

Every day provides an opportunity for learning, and our brains crave new experiences and stimulation. By taking notes or journaling, we build on what we know, but also what we don't. If you haven't tried transcribing birds onto paper, try it today. See what you can learn from this exercise.

In the following section of the book, we offer space for you to jot down some notes or sketches for each Exploration, as we share personal insights and memories on the same subject. This is just a starting point, and we hope it will encourage you to reflect and explore further in your own personal voyage of discovery.

Learning to Look #1

Sometimes it's hard to keep it simple. In birding and so many other things in life we are conditioned to give things a name, put it in a box or we have to have the right answer. These are not the things that are important to me. I would simply ask, "What do I see?" When I get back to these basics, this is when I really slow down and get lost in nature. There is no right or wrong. You see, it's all about the question, not the answer — it's that journey of discovery that is the fun.
- Richard

Getting Closer to Birds #2

I had to buy a camera and big, fancy (and very heavy) lens for Co-authoring The Shorebird Guide. A couple of top photographers gave me grief for doing it wrong: I dumped the tripod and flash. With less gear, I could get down low; even getting in the water with the birds. Lying still, quietly and with movements in slow motion, birds would soon be feeding all around me. Getting older, yes, I've become lazier; standing taller and drier, I no longer get that closeness and eye-level intimacy. I need to get back to down and dirty... - Richard

In the Moment: Are You a Pioneer? #3

Birding is almost unrecognizable today. Time, technology and DNA have completely changed our understanding. I often try to escape everything, sit quietly and ask myself questions. Are my garden Carolina Chickadees really resident? If so, where do their offspring go and how far? If they move to find a territory, are they really resident? Research found that in the hybrid Carolina X Black-capped Chickadee zone, it's the smaller Carolina that impregnates the larger Black-capped. This zone has moved north with climate change. We barely know our common birds. Perhaps you will be the next chickadee pioneer — we know so little and I love that... - Richard

Bringing Birds To You #4

The closer we are to nature, the more we love it. I started in nature looking for eggs, then birds; I got binoculars, then a scope and now I am naked without a camera. What am I? 'Confused' is probably the best answer. I love tools that allow me to be a voyeur of nature. Today the camera and other tools are bringing a new era of nature lovers. I'm on my third life! Not sure how many more I will have...
- Richard

Watching Closely: Backyard Drama #5

I bet you have also done it - sat there in a crowd, quietly watching as people move by. You see how tall they are, if they need to lose a bit of weight and how they move. They move by and you might even watch them from behind. Their clothes and colors change; but that's not the focus, it's their size, shape and movement. Yes, I am a voyeur. I love watching and working things out but rarely with people, always for birds. The game is the same for both; the feathered subjects are just much more fascinating to me. - Richard

The Jigsaw Puzzle #6

I was brought up in the young and passionate British birding scene. You were expected to take field notes; no guides allowed! Quickly, I started to see so much more. More importantly, I started to notice the small nuances of behavior, variation and other traits. Simply put, they opened up and trained me for a new world of discovery. Today, my note books (journaling was not in the English language back then) are prized possessions. They are part of my history — they shaped me to be more observant in all aspects of life; and those priceless memories...
- Richard

Recording Life #7

Years ago, I started carrying a long-lens camera wherever I go in the natural world. I'm not a photographer in the true sense of the word but love the ability to capture moments in nature that unfold around me. I use this tool as opportunity to learn and revisit - like a souvenir from a cherished moment. I record birdsongs, calls, and other sounds outdoors with my iPhone. This provides understanding and further thinking about sounds heard from that moment. Recording life around me enhances my experiences in a multi-dimensional way - extending my moments with birds just a bit longer. - Holly

Cortisol and Nature #8

The heartbeat of nature has stirred in my soul as long as I can remember. As a child, I self-medicated attention deficit through distractions in nature. Exploration outdoors is limitless and filled with discovery. If I'm feeling stressed by the weight of the world, I open my door and step into nature. I'm instantly soothed by the smells, sounds, and possibilities. A walk through the forest synchronizes my heart with the world around me. The song of the Wood Thrush rings in my mind, carrying my worries away, as it floats up into the air. - Holly

Taking A Walk #9

When I go on a walk, I set the goal of hoping to be surprised by what I see, hear, and find in nature. For me, nature is full of constant surprises, and I look forward to what I'll pull out of the "goodie bag" each time I start walking and tuning in. For me, tuning in means being in the moment. I give myself the permission to focus, to detach from my life for a few minutes-a guilty pleasure. I absorb myself in seeking both the new and familiar, and learning new things by observation.
- Holly

Know What You Know #10

I find myself taking for granted some of the common birds around me. What am I missing? A lot. I'm often distracted by trying to take it all in, versus careful study of the familiar. I pretend I'm looking at a bird I've seen a thousand times with new eyes, like I've never seen it before. When I allow myself to do this, I start to really see it. I notice subtle nuances in the way it moves, or how it feeds. I learn this bird in a new way. And in turn, I become a better observer. - Holly

Tuning Out While Tuning In #11

Closing my eyes and just listening brings me closer to nature. Allowing my brain to tune into only sounds grounds me in the moment. I can feel myself start to relax. This type of quiet puts me into a state of mindfulness. Experiencing natural soundscapes is exhilarating - as if nature's secrets are being whispered into my ears. I savor the sounds I hear that much more. Sounds become bolder, brighter, and sweeter - as if the volume's been turned up just for me. I hear more, and I connect myself to the world in a more intimate way. - Holly

Meditation 1: Appreciating Our Breath

After I started practicing meditation and mindfulness, I realized that our breath is so important! It can be slow when we are relaxed or speed up when we get excited. Whenever I go with my dad to hunt down a rare bird, I can always tell when we are getting close because his breathing will speed up. Even during moments like this we can remember to focus on our breath and enjoy the present moment. Finding a rare bird is something we always want to remember well, so don't forget to breathe! - Sophie

Behavior #12

It should be called voyeurism, not behavior. Birds, just like us, have patterns of behavior. Watching and understanding them is the most underappreciated aspect of nature watching. For me, it is the most fascinating, and also incredibly helpful in knowing who they are. Think food and breeding, and it all makes more sense. Nothing in nature is by accident. It is logical. So, think like a bird and it will put a smile on your face. - Richard

Finding Diversity #13

Diversity in nature is what brings me excitement. Nature distracts me in the best possible way. I've been drawn to it as long as I can remember. The smells, sounds, and feel of nature bring joy and drive my life forward. I look at the world as one big living organism - all parts linked together. I'm awestruck by the moth nectaring in my garden. With a flashlight, I see its eyeshine spark in the dark of night. It's linked to the flower, me, and the Eastern Phoebe that finds it, in the early morning light. - Holly

Color in Nature #14

"Color is the root of all evil." There, I just said it. Please don't hate me. When IDing birds, size, shape, behavior and sound are more important; like with people. These are consistent; color is not. Think of color in shades of gray; patterns of color are consistent. I love color, too. I am fascinated by how owls, grouse and other cryptic birds get grey, rufous, or a mixture of both, feathers. How are these colors selected? When I hope someday my research will show Darwin's natural selection theory is only a part of the big picture. The use of color by birds is the endless unknown. Oh, how I love that! - Richard

Seeing Red: The Laws of Attraction #15

How can you ignore the red in a Scarlet Tanager? You are right, you can't. However, when it comes to bird ID, people always start with color. It is like IDing me from the color of my skin. Doing it with birds is equally futile. Watch the basics of size, shape and behavior, and then enjoy the brilliance of the color. Then, try to think of it in shades of gray, as if you were color blind. - Richard

Adaptations #16

When I'm looking at a bird's bill, I imagine it as a tool that is carefully constructed to help it eat exactly what it needs to in order to survive. I liken the shape to recognizable objects: a triangle, a carrot, needle-nose pliers...When I do this, it helps me understand how the bird might use its bill, and remember it later, if I'm trying to make an identification. For example: it makes sense that a bird with a long dagger-like bill might be used to spear fish- like a heron or egret.- Holly

Goldfinches #17

Watching an American Goldfinch in flight makes me smile. They seem so gleeful as they bounce up and down, skipping through the sky, calling their "potato-chip" songs. They make flying look fun, not just purposeful. I admit, I sometimes imagine I'm that goldfinch I'm watching. Carefree and just moving through the air... - Holly

Thinking Inside the Box #18

I love to challenge myself to look at nature from the macro-level. Finding small patches to confine my exploration allows me the "insider's" look to unseen terrain and habitat. An ultimate challenge in discovery. Like using a giant magnifying glass to see the world through the eyes of an ant, I feel like a kid again, filled with wonder. Sometimes I find teeny-tiny flowers on "weeds" in my grass. Miniature beauties, unseen, forgotten and unnoticed. In these moments, I feel I'm the luckiest person alive, as I delight in the new, which was always there just waiting to be discovered. - Holly

Hummingbirds #19

Fresh off the boat, summer in NJ was too hot for an English boy. This was your typical hot sticky day. I watched this super-sized insect whizz past me. I watched it fly 80 yards down the track before I realized that was my first ever hummingbird. I had never seen anything like it – hummers are only in the Americas. That was 1985 and I still remember it like yesterday. Since then I have seen around 100 species of hummingbird. Their iridescent colors, crazy tails and crests are insane. For me though, it is their behavior that I love, particularly how they interact with one another. We could learn a lot from them! - Richard

Connections to the World Above Us #20

When I look into the sky, I let myself get lost in the vastness. I am also waiting to be thrilled at any second by something interesting that might fly by! I'm always looking for birds above - watching them wing their way past. I wonder to myself: where are they going? How long have they been aloft? I might see a migratory bird who could be on a non-stop journey that can take several days before hitting land. This is a wondrous feat, and I feel privileged to watch even a second of its journey towards its next destination. - Holly

Nuthatches #21

I was 14 when I accompanied my dad to look at a small farm that was for sale. It was a beautiful day and there it was, the Nuthatch. I had never seen a nuthatch; I was blown away. Spiffy looking and with attitude, it was walking head-first down the trunk of a tree. Of course, when my dad asked what I thought about the place, it got a big thumbs-up. Life was going to be good living around these birds. Well, my Dad and I were wrong about buying the place; but I never got tired of watching nuthatches. Life decisions, to this day, start and finish with birds. - Richard

Meditation 2: Mindful Movement

One of my favorite things to do in a city is sit down on a park bench and watch everything move around me. There are loads of people buzzing about: some strolling through the park, some zipping speedily to work, and others stumbling around in circles while holding a map. Birds are the same way! Some flit about beneath picnic tables searching for crumbs. Others sit atop poles and survey the area below. When we sit still and just observe, it's amazing to see how much is actually moving around us... - Sophie

Food For Thought #22

Bringing the birds in closer with feeders brings joy, offering me a front-row seat to a constantly shifting cast of characters. I'm always thrilled when someone new comes to the feast, or makes a seasonal debut. Inviting birds in to my nature's bounty dinner party, by designing my summer and fall yard-scape with flowers in mind to bring in my feathered friends, adds a certain thrill. My favorite plants are the sages I pot for hummingbirds, dining on the wing of migration in late summer and fall- a brilliant last gasp of summer held in a tiny package with wings and feathers. - Holly

Doves #23

The Passenger Pigeon was probably the most common bird in the world in the 1800's. Flocks of 100,000's were reported. Killed en masse, they were all but extinct in two decades. We now know that this mass of birds was critical to its survival; once below the still significant threshold, they were doomed for extinction. The folks in the Great Plains did not know that. We do now – well, some do... - Richard

Weathering #24

When I was 13, I spent a summer at sailing camp. One of the first things they taught us was how to tell which direction the wind is coming from. Funnily enough, the birds always seemed to know! Just like boats, birds face into the direction of the wind. I also noticed that when it's cold, some birds only stand on one leg - no point in having two cold feet if you can just stand on one! Even though I was at sailing camp, you could say I learned just as much about the birds that were around. - Sophie

Nature's Music Therapy #25

My memories of playing on the beach as a kid are always paired with the chattering of 'seagulls' in the background. It sounds like home, despite the notoriously pesky gulls sneaking in for a bite from my food. They seem to chatter to each other in a way that sounds like they're laughing at me because they stole my food, which is presumably why they're called Laughing Gulls. Still, their 'laughter' fills me with fond memories of summers spent by the beach. - Sophie

Meditation 3: Soundscape Surroundings

There are only a few sounds that I am highly tuned into, like when my phone goes off or someone says my name. As for the rest, it can be hard to focus on so many sounds at once! To take a break from city or work noise, I like to go for a walk on the beach. Yes, there is still noise, but a very different kind! I can hear the 'laughter' of gulls, the breeze rustling the dunes, waves lapping the shore, and even the occasional lifeguard whistle in the summer. There is so much to hear if we just stop to listen. - Sophie

Feathers #26

I love finding feathers on the ground, allowing closer looks, to appreciate subtle color nuances or iridescence, normally not seen while the feather adorns the bird. When I happen upon a stray feather, it's like a surprise gift left behind, just for me. I study its design, and how it feels against my skin as I touch it. And, I imagine: what would it be like to be covered in the soft armor of feathers? If I could choose my colors, would I sport a rainbow array of bold patterns, or intricate patterns that blend me into my environment? - Holly

Molt #27

In winter, the American Goldfinches in my yard fade into the muted colors of quiet landscapes. Subdued, their plumage is still recognizable in olive-gold. Each year, I gauge spring's arrival by watching the lemon yellow feathers of the males begin to appear in bright splotches. This new spring wardrobe is a partial molt. Their tail and wing feathers remain intact and sturdy and will be replaced in fall. The white wing-bars erode with wear, until the wing becomes solid black. So predictable, you can almost set your calendar by the molt pattern of a goldfinch. - Holly

Tails: A Balance of Life #28

I am always drawn to the length of a tail, and how it's shaped and patterned. I can learn a lot about how a bird maneuvers just by looking at these features. I especially take notice of a bird's tail when it's in motion. I'm looking to see if it moves, twists, turns. I've learned that birds with short tails and longer wings are faster. Birds with longer tails and shorter tails aren't adapted for speed while in flight, but still use their tails to maneuver and balance effectively for their preferred habitats. - Holly

Wrens #29

Sometimes we find birds in unexpected places. While driving the freeway, I stopped at a rest area, stepped outside my car, and heard a Pacific Wren singing from the nearby wooded edge. After a hectic day, I needed an Ornitherapy break. I walked closer to the song, and looked into the moss-laden woody landscapes. I closed my eyes, listening to that musically complex and beautiful song (one of my favorites) and just soaked the moment in. The sounds, the earthy smells coupled with fir and spruce overtones, and the sparkling wren song. The power of bird song is overwhelming. - Holly

Bird Brilliance: The Smarts of Birds #30

That a single bird can wing its way around the globe from pole to pole in a single year, while always returning to the same rock off the coast of Maine, is mind-boggling to me. An individual Arctic Tern can typically fly 44,000 miles in one year; this is amazing! How do they do it? Wandering the open ocean, from North to South America, then to Africa, and northward up and over to Maine...finding the same special rocky island on which to nest each spring. A bird's ability to navigate the globe is beyond brilliance in my mind. - Holly

Flocking #31

This spectacle beats all, bar none: to watch a huge flock is what I live for. I will travel the world to see it. I left England to live in Cape May, NJ for one reason, to watch the massive migration spectacles there. When the weather looked good, it was like Santa was coming. A sky full of migrants flying over at night telling each other the road map through chip notes. Flocks of shorebirds travel around the world to and from Tierra Del Fuego to the high-Arctic: who tells them which way to go? Starlings or skimmers move in perfect synchronized harmony; they never make a mistake. Endless miracles! - Richard

Reflections in Light #32

Photographers call it the beautiful light: the saturated reds of early and late day. We all love them. But what about looking in the harsh midday light? Personally, I love it all. Look at all types of light from every angle. It is endless fun. Looking into the sun and seeing only in shades of red or black and white, simplifies things. Suddenly it's all about shape and movement. Michael Jackson got it. In Tokyo1990, I watched him perform Smooth Criminal behind a massive screen: shape and movement in black and white. It rocked my world. Every angle is great, and often less is more. - Richard

Bluebirds #33

One year, I decided to volunteer as a bluebird trail monitor at the local park. I was responsible for monitoring 20 boxes, spread out over several acres. Each week, I'd monitor each of my boxes: examining its contents, identifying nests, counting eggs, and ultimately determining a fledging date. Sometimes the boxes held House Wrens. Other times, Tree Swallows. Occasionally, a snake! But when it held bluebirds, I took special pride in being its caretaker. The chicks became like my own children as I proudly watched them grow to fledge. I learned a lot about bluebirds, but more importantly, about stewardship. - Holly

Dusk: A Twilight Shift #34

The vivid colors of the sunset make any shapes that pass in the foreground stand out dramatically. When watching the sunset at home in New Jersey, I often see small birds flitting around in the last light of the evening. I can't always see the color or patterns of their feathers, but the setting sun outlines their shape, size, and how they move. They zig and zag all over the place, elegant but uncatchable. A lot of bugs come out at night, especially in the summer, so I think the birds are zipping around in search of dinner! - Sophie

Birds Go Straight To The Heart   #35

I love walking through urban environments to find nature thriving in unexpected places. Cracks in the sidewalks are a favorite: I love to look closely, and find tiny flowers or plants, even a blade of grass, pushing up, demonstrating the tenacity of life. Spotting a Peregrine Falcon making passes over skyscrapers is a thrill. Robins pull worms from small patches of grass next to intersections. A cardinal sings its cheer song, from a shrub next to a building. Wherever we go, we can find something new in nature. Nature's wonders fill me up. How about you? - Holly

We Are Connected #36

"Nothing in nature is by accident" – it is my favorite saying. Birds eat, drink, fly, breed and grow new feathers. These actions are all connected and nothing is ever by accident. When you realize there is a purpose to everything they do, all you need is a fair amount of common sense to work out why things are the way they are. It's all logical and I LOVE that! - Richard

Living Together #37

Travelling the world, you realize nothing is as portrayed. There is clearly no normal because everywhere is different; in values, expectations, societal norms and how we perceive ourselves. The poorer the people, the simpler the life, the happier they are; and they have nothing in common with the lust for power of the people that rule them. Living on three Continents, birding on all of them, has taken me to see the real World. It is the greatest education anyone can get. No school can teach you about real life. Current events, climate change and the internet connect us. Now I hope we can learn to look, observe, and see each other. Our lives, and those of future generations, would be so much better if we are living together. - Richard

Sparrows #38

Subtly beautiful and feisty – I like that! In winter, white-throated, Song and others (white-crowned in the west) congregate in the garden, particularly in bad weather, if I remember to stock up the feeders (yes, I do sometimes forget). They mix, so you can see their different sizes and shapes. Subtle but so beautifully patterned when you look closely. It's their behavior and how they co-mingle I really enjoy. They seem to have it sorted out but then there will be a little skirmish, words said, and then back to business. What do you think they are saying? - Richard

Staying Afloat #39

Bobbing with the soft rolls of the tide, I watch a single loon floating quietly on the bay. Its red eye glistens in the sunlight, as the emerald green of its head and neck shine like satin. Black and white herringbone jacket of feathers lays across its back like dapper haberdashery. It looks peaceful as it rests. Suddenly, it dives, slipping under the surface with grace with elegance. I wait, as I wonder when it will reappear. It bobs to the surface unannounced. Droplets of water bead on its back. It floats effortlessly. I'd like to be a loon. - Holly

Under the Surface #40

I've always been inspired by animals that are able to glide freely and comfortably below the surface of the ocean, especially birds. They have the best of both worlds! Their aerodynamic bodies and feathers make them perfectly suited to fly, but they can also have webbed feet that help propel them through the water while searching for prey. While my body isn't as naturally adapted to move in the water as some diving birds, I like to think that my freediving fins are my own way of being "dressed for the part of the salt life." - Sophie

Preening #41

When I catch a glimpse of a bird preening, I feel comforted in knowing that in this moment the bird is relaxed, and has let its guard down - if even just for a moment. As I watch, I know that this bird preens in order to take care of itself to thrive. Self-maintenance on several levels. I ask myself: am I preening each day, in order to thrive in the moment and the future? If we allow ourselves to be vulnerable, and focus on self-care, we take care of our bodies, minds, and spirits. When do you preen? - Holly

The Bug Life #42

The bugs I remember most are often the ones that catch me off guard: walking into a spider web, being bitten by a mosquito, or even pesky flies landing on my food. These are all things that a lot of people experience, and for that exact reason, can leave a bad impression of bugs. Bugs can have a bad reputation, but have you ever watched a spider spin its web? Or a bumble bee pollinate a flower? They do amazing things for the planet. Bugs may be small, but they are mighty! Take a closer look and you will see the positive massive impact of these miniscule creatures. - Sophie

Bird Feet #43

During winter as a young child, I thought many birds only had one leg and one foot. They would stand facing into the wind, cold winter air bristling their feathers, balancing on one foot. I was convinced that all of these birds only had one leg and foot, when in reality they actually lift the other up to their body to keep it warm. For some birds, their feet are a lifeline – for catching food, standing, and even swimming – so they have to keep them warm and safe during the bitter winter months. A bird's feet can tell you a lot about them! - Sophie

Camouflage #44

Finding treasures along sandy shores is a favored pastime. Walking along the beach, my eye caught movement ahead of me. Expecting a crab, instead I found myself locking eyes with a male Piping Plover. Blending perfectly into the sand, this pale and tiny shorebird seemed to disappear into the sand as he repeatedly ran then stopped, while hunting below the dunes. For him, "bleached" feathers allow a ghostly existence; a leg up in survival in the beach life. For me, I'd found a treasure I wasn't expecting - witnessing precious moments in the life of a shorebird. This is Ornitherapy. - Holly

Variability in Birds and Life #45

I got into birds when I was knee-height to a grasshopper and spent hours absorbing my 2 bird books. To this day, I remember thinking how wrong they were. Birds live in places, not on white backgrounds. They are rarely side on and they move. Birds would go from gray in winter to boldly colored in summer. Do they do this in hours I would ask? In real life it seemed like no two were alike. The books made it look so simple, yet reality was so completely different. And we wonder why people struggle sticking names on birds... - Richard

Avian Athletes: Migration Miracles #46

In Sept. 1985, fellow Englishman Paul Holt and I were fresh off the boat and 21. We were in Cape May for southbound fall migration. Everything was flying north just after daybreak — it didn't make sense. We found a great dredge spoil on Sept. 20, climbed it, and life would never be the same again for me. As the sun came up, migrants zipped over, sometimes throughyou, flying back north; sometimes in thousands. It's Space Invaders on steroids. Why are they doing it, where are they, how long do they fly and how do you ID them? My life was changed. I had to move to Cape May for good. Those migration miracles are still happening and we still don't have the answers. How remarkable is that? - Richard

The Bird's Eye View #47

Fancy thinking and seeing like a bird! We always convert things into 'human-terms'. No birds or other animals are like us — they see everything differently. When I took up serious photography in 2006, it was important to get close to birds. Crawling on the ground, no sudden movements or noises were key. I researched 'squeaking' — making harsh noises by putting your fingers to your lips. Birds came to check out the threatening noise. Interestingly different species reacted differently to this noise. How far away would they come, how close, and how responsive to other actions I make. Fascinating. They soon realized I'm not for real. Sadly, they are always less interested in me than I am in them. - Richard

Mob Rules: A Call to Attention #48

Searching for spring migrant warblers in a small park near my home, I heard the alarm calls of robins, cardinals, and chickadees. I followed the calls, and found a group of birds, all circled in one direction. I froze, and let my eyes find the target of their mobbing: it was an Eastern Screech Owl, tucked into the shadows of branches in a shrub. Finding an owl during the day is always a thrill. In this case, I wasn't the finder- I just listened to the language of birds and allowed them to steer me towards their fantastic discovery. - Holly

Bothersome Birds #49

If we are bird lovers, do we have to like all birds? Sometimes, there are behaviors of birds that drive us mad. The House Sparrow is a perfect example. I get frustrated when I find one has "won-out" the nestbox offered for my bluebirds. The House Sparrow was imported to the US in the mid 1800s, and was able to thrive here. Often aggressively outcompeting other birds, they wreak havoc in our yards. But is it havoc? Or is this nature in its boldest and most impressive form of survival? In the end, I appreciate their tenacity, and find them beautiful. - Holly

Meditation 4: Visualizing Connection

Sometimes I like to think about how many physical objects I am connected to. For example, right now as I am typing, I am touching my computer, wearing clothes that cover my body, my legs and back are on a chair and my feet are on the ground. That's 5 things I am connected to already! That doesn't even include emotional connections or connections to the environment I am in. The list goes on and on and on... What are you connected to right now? - Sophie

Nest Cavities #50

To this day, I still remember setting up bird boxes at my elementary school. I loved looking for nests and eggs in my backyard, and now we were going to have nests at my school, too! There was nothing more I wanted than to share this passion with my friends. It was priceless to know that we could help create a safe environment for birds to raise their young, especially as cities continue to envelope vital natural habitat. The young people of today are paving the way for the young birds of tomorrow. - Sophie

Aerial Insectivores #51

For centuries, man has wanted to fly like a bird. We learned to do it by copying birds. I was told Boeing Aircraft Company paid Kodak millions to film Common Grackles. It showed the trailing edge of the grackles' wings going up and down constantly, like the rudders that go up and down on take off and landing. Next time you have a wing seat on a plane, look out the window and remember it all comes from birds. - Richard

Wading Birds #52

I was never into herons and big birds. Spending time in Florida
has changed all that. The noise, smells and behavior at heronry is
something you have to do. They nest next to each other but are so
aggressive. Makes me wonder why you would live next to someone if you
are going to fight all the time. Watching the males display makes me
really think I need to up my game. As for the youngsters, they make
our kids look so sweet. Like I've said, everyone is a voyeur. - Richard

Scavengers #53

Don't you love how vultures jump around, cleaning up the mess? They get such a bad rap, perhaps because of how they are portrayed by Disney and others. I love their character and majesty in the air. Unfortunately, when I see them it always takes my mind back to when I spent several months in India in the late 80's. There were vultures everywhere (about 80 million). By the millennium, they were critically endangered and most species were in danger of extinction due to man's use of the drug diclofenac on cattle. The negative effect to the ecosystem is massive. We need vultures and other scavengers to tidy up OUR mess: They don't make one! - Richard

Apex Predators #54

Spotting a Red-tailed Hawk soaring over my yard reminds me of the balance in nature right in my own neighborhood. Does she spy the squirrel that's been raiding my feeders? Perhaps her eye is fixed on the rabbit in my neighbor's veggie garden. Where is her mate? Will she have offspring this year to continue filling the gaps in the ecological niches nearby? She soars on broad wings and fanned tail - the sun shining through the orange feathers like stained glass in the sky. She's a majestic beauty that helps keeps life in balance, as she sits atop the pyramid. - Holly

Celebrating Roles #55

Each spring, a male bluebird brings his juvenile clutch to my porch. He lines them up on a branch side-by-side, their mouths open wide. He hurries over to my feeders, over-stuffing his bill with mealworms, gobs of suet, or maybe a sunflower chip. He shovels the food into each gaping mouth. Fed one-by-one, he hopes to quiet their hungry calls. But they just beg for more. And in that same order, he repeats the paternal duties without resting. Tirelessly working, he's the perfect example of a father's devotion and love. - Holly

Celebrating Roles II #56

Just as quickly as they arrived back after winter away, a pair of Bluegray Gnatcatchers went straight to work nest-building in the notch of a tree. I first noticed the female, carrying bits of lichen into the nest, carefully placing it around the edges to secure and camouflage it within the tree. While she pulled spiderwebs into place tightening the cup, the male serenaded from a nearby tree. Upon her departure, he jumped into the nest carrying his offerings of structural security, adorning the sides with fibers, seeming to sew it all together. An act of love, or perfect teamwork? - Holly

Patterns of Color #57

Where do I start? Which is crazier, the terms of 'black' and 'white' for describing people, or that so many people try identifying birds based on color? Think of shades. People come in shades of brown and birds come in shades of gray. And yes, I will be in big trouble for saying this! Everything in life for all animals is about patterns: color, behavior; and yes, even sizes and shapes are patterns in my eyes. Patterns of color very rarely change, only the color itself. If you are not color blind, try seeing everything in fifty shades of gray for ten minutes. Everything will make more sense. - Richard

Connecting Others to Birds #58

One of the greatest gifts you can give to another person is your time. Time is our most precious commodity, and it is limited. Enriching someone's life by spending time outdoors with them, and showing them the wonders and joys of nature, fills the soul with happiness. I love showing people birds and inviting them to experience the wonder, the pleasure, and happiness in seeing something new. The joy of discovery. Of opening doors to what's right there, waiting for them, if they take the time to look. And, if they do, I hope they someday pay it forward.
 - Holly

Meditation 5: Cultivating Curiosity

I recently experienced an increase in free time, so I asked myself: what do I want to do now? This sparked a sense of curiosity not just about my interests, but about everything around me. I started thinking differently! What hobby did I want to pick up? Did I want to go for a walk outside? What did I notice outside? Why do the birds outside my house only sing in the evening? There are so many questions out there, and we can only discover the answer by asking... - Sophie

Your Ornitherapy

Everyone experiences Ornitherapy differently. We lead unique lives with unique experiences and observations of the world around us. We have left these pages blank for you to use as you are inspired.